The Weaver, the Word and Wisdom

The Weaver, the Word and Wisdom

Worshipping the Triune God

Michaela Youngson

Copyright © 2007 Michaela Youngson
Cover Image: Creation by Denise Wheeler 2007
Photo by Sandy Youngson 2007
Background image © PureStockX

British Library Cataloguing in Publication data
A catalogue record for this book is available
from the British Library

ISBN 978-1-905958-07-8

First published by Inspire
4 John Wesley Road
Werrington
Peterborough PE4 6ZP

Printed and bound in Great Britain by
Stanley L Hunt (Printers) Ltd, Rushden, Northants.

This book is dedicated to
all those who long for the
Church truly to reflect the
inclusive love of God.

Acknowledgements

Denise Wheeler for her wonderful paintings and textiles.

Sandy, Robert and Tamsin for everything.

Cathy Bird, Lorraine Brown, Dorlis Hirshbul and Lucy Winkett for space, time, coffee, wine, Scrabble and cake!

Natalie Watson and Lorna Valentine at Inspire.

Contents

Introduction

To worship God is to worship the whole of God. Yet what human being can grasp the full being and reality of God? Christians have recognized in God a complexity that our minds cannot comprehend and yet have sought to describe the divine being within the limits of human language and concept. The myriad ways in which God chooses to be revealed to human beings become clear through the pages of Holy Scripture and have led systematic theologians and the doctrine shapers of the Early Church to that most extraordinary metaphor, the Trinity. Christians are invited into a relationship with God who is recognized in three persons, dancing in perichoresis (mutual indwelling), eternally living in relationship. To even contemplate removing one person from the whole is nonsense, because there are no clear lines dividing one from the other. Father, Son and Holy Spirit, or Creator, Redeemer, Sustainer, are not separate beings, rather they are ways of God being.

When I began this book it was partly a response to the number of times I have heard preachers declare that given a choice they would rather not preach on Trinity Sunday because it is such a difficult doctrine to preach about. While having sympathy that getting one's head around the idea of the Trinity is challenging, I find myself delighted at the opportunity to explore this central idea at the heart of Christian theology. Not for one moment because I think I have this idea sorted out and can neatly deliver the perfect sermon, but because however deeply I dig into the idea, I never reach the end.

This book is divided into three sections, each focusing particularly on a 'person' of the Trinity, but it is impossible to divide God neatly in this way. To talk about the Creator is meaningless without reference to the Word. Our understanding of the reality of God is distorted if we fail to recognize the Spirit as active in all time. So each section of this book attempts not to separate the persons of God, but to bring into focus one facet of the Trinity, while recognizing that the wholeness of God is present at all times.

The metaphors we explore or create lead us deeper into the tangled, interwoven, eternally complex person of God. As the body, spirit and personality of a human being cannot be divided without losing the whole, so our attempts to separate God into manageable pieces are set to fail.

I have found myself surprised by how often the metaphor of water has come to the fore within these chapters, particularly when exploring the idea of the 'Word of God'. My initial instinct was to link water and Spirit, yet on reflection it is the penetrating Word of God that shapes creation as water shapes the landscape over and through which it flows. The Word that dances through our understanding of Wisdom existed at the beginning of all things and, as Spirit, the breath of God continues to move in creation and human lives today.

I believe that our worship needs to be linked with the way we live, and our actions in the world. We do not earn salvation through our deeds but through the generous grace of God. The only appropriate response to that grace is to pay attention to the people we become. Each chapter within this book contains suggestions for practical actions that link to the themes of worship offered.

It has been a great privilege to work with Denise Wheeler, a new talent in the Christian art world. Her paintings and textile pieces interpret her spiritual experience and her glimpses of God. The cover image and those within this book were in response to Denise's reading of the text. It is a strange and thrilling experience to see how an artist visually interprets ideas first described in words. There is something of the mutual dance of the Trinity in the relationship between word, image, artist and writer that has developed through this book.

I hope that the worship resources and reflections in *The Weaver, the Word and Wisdom* help you to explore your own relationship with God and offer material that you might use in leading worship. Each chapter ends with a poem that is not necessarily written with public worship in mind. These tend to be my own personal response to a theme or issue that has arisen and are a glimpse of who I am. In the end, regardless of the doctrines of the Church, we come before God as we are. As we celebrate the Trinity, we celebrate ourselves, made in the image of God.

The Weaver, the Word and Wisdom

In the beginning, the Weaver, the Word and Wisdom
moving in relationship together,
caught a vision of potential,
a glimpse of possibility, and
with tentative steps, creation's dance began.

Creation was shot through with the generosity of the Weaver's grace.
The rhythm of life's passion played loudly
as a constant beat at the heart of myriad universes.

Against this universal backdrop the Word moved
and became free, small and intimate.
In the cry of a child, the song of a woman
and the shout of a dying man
the Word's voice added melody to the Weaver's song.

In the midst of confusion, absence and loss,
Wisdom found her way.
She had danced with the Weaver's threads, throughout all time,
weaving a maypole dance of energetic passion.
She added harmony to the beat and the melody
and composed a symphony of colour.

If creation for a single moment fails to hear the Weaver's rhythm,
or misses the Word's intimate melody,
then Wisdom will dance through the silence
until all that is joins in love's rejoicing.

The Rock

Creation echoes

Creation echoes

Genesis 1.1–5 and John 1.1–5

In the beginning was the Word, and the Word was with God, and the Word was God.

In the beginning when God created the heavens and the earth, the earth was a formless void and darkness covered the face of the deep, while a wind from God swept over the face of the waters.

He was in the beginning with God. All things came into being through him, and without him not one thing came into being.

Then God said, 'Let there be light'; and there was light. And God saw that the light was good.

What has come into being in him was life, and the life was the light of all people.

And God separated the light from the darkness. God called the light Day, and the darkness he called Night. And there was evening and there was morning, the first day.

The light shines in the darkness, and the darkness did not overcome it.

(To be read by two voices)

Mystical hints

Reflection

The strands of God's identity weave together in the blending of these creation stories. John offers the reader mystical and metaphysical hints to the mystery of the Word, Jesus, being with God and actually being God at the beginning of all things.

John reads between the lines of the Genesis tale, going beyond the external and physical elements of the creation story. He draws from what to him would be a familiar tale, deeper truths about the nature of God and the true identity of Jesus Christ. Here, 'in the beginning' of his telling of the story, John makes the most outrageous claim, not only that Jesus has been part of God since creation, but that without Jesus creation would not have been possible.

It is the power of an intimate, loving, mutual relationship that makes creation possible. The love at the heart of God created life and offers hope for the re-creation of life. We who call ourselves 'the body of Christ' enter into that creative relationship and become co-creators with God. Our discipleship places a responsibility upon us to be part of the renewing and restoring of creation.

So are we to work towards a global utopia where there is no hardship, pain or suffering? Can we return to Eden and bask in endless light? I find myself unconvinced that the innocence of mythical Eden offers a past reality or a helpful future hope. The writers of Genesis and John draw distinctions between darkness and light, but both still exist. Darkness has not overcome light; each has its part to play in the experience of human beings. John's vision is not of a naive creation, it is a place where people reject good, even failing to recognize God's Son. Human life is a place where mistakes are made, where the sharpest point of God's engaging with the world is missed. Yet it is also a place were we can see God's glory, as of a parent's only child, full of grace and truth.

Praise our Creator

Adoration

Creator God,
maker of all that is, we offer you our praise:
Heaven and earth are full of your glory.

You brought light out of darkness,
day for our fulfilment and night for our rest:
Heaven and earth are full of your glory.

You raised the mountains, laid low the plains,
filled the seas with life and sprinkled the sky with stars:
Heaven and earth are full of your glory.

You formed people; children, women and men,
diverse, complex, creative and beautiful:
Heaven and earth are full of your glory.

You did not abandon us to chaos,
but remain intimately involved in our story:
Heaven and earth are full of your glory.

You revealed your love in the life of your Son,
your Word made flesh, living among us:
Heaven and earth are full of your glory.

You move within our lives as Holy Spirit,
opening our eyes to your grace and truth.
Heaven and earth are full of your glory.

Creator God,
maker of all that is, we offer you our praise:
Heaven and earth are full of your glory.

Accept our praise in Christ's name.
Amen.

Forgive us for not treading gently

Confession

Creator God, your world is full of beauty and diversity.
Through actions of violence and attitudes of ignorance
we have made it ugly and demanded conformity:
Forgive us for not treading gently on sacred ground.

Creator God, all we have is born of love.
Through actions of hate and attitudes of prejudice
we have learned to see our neighbours as dangerous and evil:
Forgive us for not treading gently on sacred ground.

Creator God, you have given us more than we can ever need.
Through actions of greed and attitudes of carelessness
we have deprived our neighbours of your good gifts:
Forgive us for not treading gently on sacred ground.

In silence we remember ways in which we have marred creation and hurt our neighbours.

God says, 'Behold, I am making all things new.'
Know in your hearts that your sins are forgiven.

Thanks be to God.
Amen.

Giver of life and light

Intercession

Giver of life and light,
we pray for places in creation where your light struggles to break through.
For places of poverty, degradation and despair:
for children who go hungry,
for women trafficked into sexual slavery,
for men taking their own lives because life seems hopeless:

**Help us to remember that the light shines in the darkness,
and the darkness will not overcome it.**

Giver of life and light,
We pray for places in creation where your light struggles to break through.
For places of suffering, sadness and fear:
for those who face ill health,
for those who live with deep grief,
for those whose future seems bleak and uncertain:

**Help us to remember that the light shines in the darkness,
and the darkness will not overcome it.**

Giver of life and light,
we pray for places in creation where your light struggles to break through.
For places of power, corruption and oppression:
that the leaders of nations will have wisdom and mercy,
that massive money-making companies will be fair to their workers,
that those who are not free to live, love or believe in their own way will know peace:

**Help us to remember that the light shines in the darkness,
and the darkness will not overcome it.**

Giver of life and light,
we pray for places in creation where your light struggles to break through.
We remember those places and people known to us who need your light and love.

Silence

**Help us to remember that the light shines in the darkness,
and the darkness will not overcome it.
In the name of God, Creator, Redeemer, Sustainer, we pray.
Amen.**

Love's spark

Hymn

In empty space, devoid of light,
a spark of love began to form.
What myriad worlds could it ignite,
what great potential might be born?
This universe of love broke through,
to God of all, our praise is due.

Love's spark moved on its living dance,
spread stars and planets in its wake,
warmed human hearts and took a chance,
that we would love's direction take.
This universe of love broke through,
to God of all, our praise is due.

When all seemed lost and love burnt low,
God breathed upon the flame again.
The Word restored love's saving glow,
and gave up life to make love plain.
This universe of love broke through,
to God of all, our praise is due.

Love's fire burned stronger than before,
defeating death, restoring light.
The Spirit blazes all the more,
replacing fear with deep insight.
This universe of love breaks through,
to God of all, our praise is due.

(Tune: 888888 Abingdon)

Creation affirmation

We believe in God
who created all things.

We believe in Jesus
through whom all things were created.

We believe in the Holy Spirit
who works continually to restore creation.

Amen.

Creation benediction

May the light of the Creator shine upon you.
May the Word of Christ call to you.
May the Spirit of God inspire you.

Amen.

Worship setting ideas

If possible, darken the worship space. Use candles for lighting, gradually lighting more candles as the service continues.

Have a white screen set up. When the passage proclaims, 'God said, "Let there be light"', project on to it the shadow of a cut-out of the world.

Action ideas

Can your church help people who want to recycle but can't get to appropriate recycling points? Lay on a weekly transport run collecting recycling from the housebound.

Find out details of Eco-Congregation (see page 143). Is this something your church community could get involved with?

Commit yourself to caring for God's world. Try simple ways such as:

Turn down your central heating thermostat by one degree.

Set your washing machine to 30 degrees for all washes.

Walk to church/work/school instead of driving.

Reduce, recycle and reuse.

Weird, wild and wonderful words

Words have a life all their own.
Beguiling, begetting,
beginning again to grasp, gasp,
gaze at the craft that carves creation.

Weird, wild and wonderful
words initiate, inspire, and
induce states of ecstasy, earache and
echoes of memory, mourning and mayhem.

Weary, woeful and wishful
words released reluctantly,
recklessly leaving love's labour's lost
and candour's damage deftly dealt.

The Word, though, what of that?
Life-creating, life-saving, life-fulfilling
eternal energy engaged with
all creation's caring and caressing.

Heavenly, holy,
heavy with sacred, sanctifying,
searing power to cleanse, to clarify
complex points of truth and theology.

Word without walls,
breaking free from frail failure,
breaking death's damning door,
and rising, running and rejoicing.

Wonderfully made

Wonderfully made

Based on Psalm 139

My Lover, you know everything about me.
You are concerned with each of my actions and understand my thoughts.
You do not wait for me to find you,
but you look for me and walk with me.
You are with me as I sleep and you know all that I do.
I need not say a word; you know what I am thinking.
You hold me and protect me, surrounding me and caressing me.
I cannot take this in, this knowledge you have of me.

Your Spirit is always with me; I cannot hide from you or run from you.
In the highest ecstasies of heavenly joy – you are there.
When I visit dark places of despair – you are there.
If I fly on the wings of morning light, and travel to the ends of the earth,
beyond the limits of my imagination – you are there.
Your hand leads me and you keep me safe.

When I despair, saying,
'The darkness overwhelms me and light will not return',
even darkness is not dark to you.
The night shines with the brilliance of the noonday sun,
for between light and dark you make no distinction.

You created each part of me, the hidden and the visible.
You crafted me and formed me as I grew in my mother's womb.
I praise you, for I am painstakingly and wonderfully made.
I see signs of your work in all creation.
While I grew in secret, I was not hidden from you.
DNA, cells, limbs and organs, intricately woven in the depths of the earth.

You could see me when I was a clutch of microscopic cells
and even then you knew the person I would become.
I cannot begin to grasp the measure of your thoughts, my Lover!
They cannot be counted; they are more than each grain of sand.
If I reach the end of all there is, I am still with you.

There are people of hatred in your world, bloodthirsty and powerful.
Can you who are so powerful not rid the world of these who lift themselves
above other people and even above you?
Help me not to hate those who despise your ways.
My instinct is to despise those who see the world differently from myself.
I make them my enemies; look at me, my Lover, read my heart.

Why test me when you know my thoughts?
If there is wickedness within me,
replace it with a desire for love and lead me in the way to life.

I put the dark on!

Reflection

I could hear my daughter playing with the light-pull in my bedroom. After a few minutes her smiling face peered round the bathroom door as she announced, 'It's all right, Mummy, I've put the dark on.' Tamsin was about two years old and had already developed a capacity for seeing the world in a unique way. After laughing for some time, I reflected on the idea of 'putting the dark on'. We talk about turning the light on and off, but not the dark. I was reminded of the words in Psalm 139 that to God 'the darkness is as light'.

This psalm can feel very comforting or very disturbing. How do we feel about the idea that God knows everything about us, our words before we have spoken, our thoughts before they have formed in our minds? This can be greatly reassuring, a promise of protection, guidance and company on our journey through life. It can also leave us uneasy, reminding us that there is nowhere that we can hide from God. God knows our actions, even those we might choose to undertake beneath the cover of darkness.

This psalm is not describing God as a cosmic police officer who sees our misdemeanours. God is well aware of our actions but, like a loving parent, this means our Creator is also able to celebrate our positive deeds. There is a deeper knowledge here, however, a knowledge that goes back to the beginning of all creation. In a similar way to the opening of John's Gospel, we are drawn in our imaginations to a time before time. 'When I was being made in secret, intricately woven in the depths of the earth.' More striking even than the idea that God knit us together in the womb, this hints at the immortality that God invites us to enter into. Before the mountains, the trees, the oceans, before life as any human being has experienced it, God had insight into the person that each of us would be.

God's activity in creation is to paint the big picture – to stretch out the heavens like a curtain (Isaiah 40.22), but also to be intimately involved in the minuscule detail of each part of that creation. Such knowledge may be too much for us, as it was for the psalmist – yet like the psalmist we are inspired to praise our Creator.

From the moment before time began

Adoration

Creator God,
immortal, intimate and imaginative,
your breath brings life to all creation,
your spark of love is at the heart of each atom:
With all creation we offer you our praise.

From the moment before time began,
you have loved and known each person here.
You have been concerned with our thoughts, words and actions:
With all creation we offer you our praise.

There is not an hour when you abandon us.
You are constant: loving, protecting and guiding us.
You are wise beyond our knowing:
With all creation we offer you our praise.

To you the darkness and light are the same.
You see, love and understand your children night and day.
We are painstakingly and wonderfully made:
With all creation we offer you our praise.

Creator God, accept our praise.
Amen.

For those times . . .

Confession

God, my Creator,
for those times when I have tried to hide my thoughts,
words and actions from you:
Forgive me and renew your Spirit within me.

For those times when I have thought myself beyond your care:
Forgive me and renew your Spirit within me.

For those times when I have forgotten
that I am wonderfully made in your image:
Forgive me and renew your Spirit within me.

For those times when I have allowed hate and prejudice
to dictate my thoughts, words and actions:
Forgive me and renew your Spirit within me.

Silence

In the confidence of the wonderful knowledge that God
will forgive our sins, we say:

Thanks be to God.
Amen.

Confident of God's concern

Intercession

In the confidence of God's concern for the smallest detail of human living, we offer our prayers for the world and ourselves.

We pray for those who find themselves in despair today:
> people who have no sense of
> > their own value,
> people who have no confidence
> > in the future,
> people who suffer the effects and
> > stigma of mental illness.

Silence

God of grace:
Hear our prayer.

We pray for those whose days are formed of fear and longing:
> parents who have no food for
> > their children,
> children who live in war zones and
> > places of conflict,
> carers who long for a break and a rest.

Silence

God of grace:
Hear our prayer.

We pray for those whose thoughts are too weighty to bear:
> people living with the guilt of a past action,
> people living with the shock of a
> > difficult diagnosis,
> people living with the burden of grief.

Silence

God of grace:
Hear our prayer.

We pray for those in our church and community who need comfort:
> ....
> ....
> ....

Silence

God of grace:
Hear our prayer.

We pray for ourselves. Help us to remember we are wonderfully made:
> teach us to rely on your presence and
> > to see signs of your glory,
> teach us to replace hate with love,
> > and fear with knowledge,
> teach us to care for others as you
> > care for us.

Silence

God of grace:
Hear our prayer.
Amen.

21

Who can reach the end of love?

Hymn

How can* we grasp the thoughts of God,
numbered more than grains of sand?
Can it be true that one so good,
has the grace to understand,
sees our falling and our rising,
knows our thoughts and shares our pain;
soars upon the wings of morning,
joins us in the depths again?

Beyond the* boundaries of this world,
even there God joins our dance.
The folds* of night become unfurled,
dark and light invite God's glance.
Deep within our mothers' wombs
God formed bodies, souls and minds,
in our hearts creating room,
love a welcome there to find.

Wonderful are your works, O God,
beyond price your gift of grace.
Nothing* is hidden, bad or good,
none is lost from your embrace.
Who can count love's every action?
Who can reach the end of love?
So we praise with deep conviction,
God, whose name is always love.

(Tune: 87 87 D, Blaenwern)

(*indicates extra note should be sung for best tune fit)

We believe . . .

Affirmation

We believe in God,
creator and parent,
lover and friend.

We believe in God,
with us on our journey,
guide and protector.

We believe in God,
painstakingly forming us
before time began.

We believe in God,
Alpha and Omega,
beginning and end.

We believe in God,
with us, Emmanuel,
caught up in our story.

We believe in God,
poured out for us,
crucified, risen, ascended.

We believe in God,
Spirit and counsellor,
inspiring generous living.

We believe in God,
moving among us,
dancing within us.

We believe in God,
intimate and holy,
joyful bringer of peace.

God's passionate care

Blessing

May God who knows you intimately
and cares for you passionately,
bless you and lead you into the way of everlasting life.

Amen.

Worship setting ideas

Place a large, low bowl full of sand as a focus in the worship space. Ask people to take some sand in their hands and try to count the number of grains.

Project on to a screen ultrasound scan images of a baby in the womb. Alternatively display an image of a tiny baby held in a hand. Be sensitive to the fact that there may be people present who might find these images distressing.

Collect a large number of images of people, showing faces young and old, of different colours, different occupations etc. Ask people to pick one and to think about the person and reflect on Psalm 139. Focus on the idea that we are 'painstakingly and wonderfully made' by God.

Action ideas

Think of anyone in your neighbourhood or community who may suffer from low self-esteem. Is there a need your church can meet? You might want to consider a drop-in for single parents, an after-school club for young people, a luncheon club for older people. Are there ways you can show that God loves each and every person?

The end of Psalm 139 contains some difficult verses about hate, particularly hatred of those who do not speak of God in the way the psalmist does. What actions can you take to overcome prejudice in your own life and in your community? Make an effort to get to know other faith communities in your town or village. Try to find out more about what people of other faiths believe. When you see prejudice on television, such as stereotypes of particular groups of people, don't just mutter – write and complain!

A mind not so dull

It is easy to forget that
I am wonderfully made.
Glancing in the mirror I see
the unkindness of time,
the unkemptness of my hair,
the uncomfortable reality of wrinkles.

It is easy to forget that
I am wonderfully made.
Climbing the stairs is no
longer a two-at-a-time race,
I'm just glad if I get to the place
without being too red in the face!

It is easy to forget that
I am wonderfully made.
Trying to remember that
phone number, PIN number, house number,
Mum's postcode, brother's birthday
and why I went upstairs in the first place.

It is easy to forget that
I am wonderfully made.
Such knowledge is a bit of a stretch
when gravity is winning the battle
and chronology the war
as I lose another set of keys.

It is easy to forget that
I am wonderfully made.
Yet I bore you, my children,
carried you in my womb,
fed you with life-giving milk
and love you with blazing passion.

It is easy to forget that
I am wonderfully made.
Yet, in all honesty, this mind is not so dull,
this body has loved and still
has occasion to know passion
and the joy of the sun on its skin.

27

Called by name

A canticle of God's creation

Isaiah 40.21–31

Has it not been told to you from the beginning?
Have you not understood from the foundations of the earth?

It is God who sits above the circle of the earth
and its inhabitants are as small as grasshoppers.

Who stretches out the heavens like a curtain
and spreads them like a tent to live in?

Who brings presidents and princes to naught
and makes the rulers of the earth as nothing?

Scarcely are they planted, scarcely are they sown,
hardly has their stem taken root in the earth,

When God blows upon them, and they wither
and like dry grass they fly before the storm.

To whom, then, will you compare me?
Who is my equal? says the Holy One.

Lift up your eyes.
Look up and see. Who created these?

God, who calls out their people and counts them,
calls each one by name:

Because God is great in strength and mighty in power,
not one is missing or left behind.

Why do you say, O Jacob,
and speak, O Israel,

'My way is hidden from God.
My right is ignored by Yahweh'?

Have you not known?
Have you not heard?

Yahweh is the everlasting God,
the Creator of the ends of the earth.

God does not faint or grow weary:
Yahweh's understanding is unsearchable.

God gives power to the faint
and strength to the powerless.

Even youths will faint and be weary,
and the young will fall exhausted:

But those who wait for God shall renew their strength.
They shall mount up with wings like eagles.

They shall run and not be weary,
they shall walk and not grow faint.

*(A helpful tradition when reading a canticle is that half the congregation
reads the first line of the couplet, and the other half reads the second line)*

A counsel not to despair

Reflection

The writer of Isaiah 40 takes great pains to remind the people of Israel of the full majesty of God the Creator. In wonderful poetry he writes of God 'who stretches out the heavens like a curtain, and spreads them like a tent to live in'. This same God who created them is far more powerful and longer lasting than the rulers of the earth. Those who are oppressing the people of Israel are nothing to God – they will wither and like dry grass will be carried off when the wind blows.

I found this particularly helpful at a time when powerful nations of the world were planning to invade Iraq. Of course, knowing that such rulers are only temporary and that the times we live in are a blink in the eye of God's eternity could lead to a fatalistic cynicism. Such knowledge does not lessen the devastating effects of war, or remove the Christian's responsibility to make a stand against things we believe are evil. In fact I find this passage leads not to cynical despair but to hope. If I believe that in the end God will restore creation and that the current order will pass away, then I have nothing to lose. Standing up for the things I believe in is more possible when I know that I am caught up in an eternal relationship of love that exists beyond the physical reality I currently inhabit.

To add to this hope and confidence in God's hold on the 'bigger picture', Isaiah introduces another idea. God knows each one of us – in fact, each of us is called by name. Not just known as part of a particular group, religion, nation, army, but as an individual. Not only does God know us, but this same God who never grows weary is able to give strength to the powerless. Those who have confidence in the Creator God, who respond to the call to faithful living, will find their strength renewed. They 'shall mount up with wings like eagles, run and not be weary'.

We are not called to despair, but to faithful and courageous living. We may not have a grasp of the full picture – that is God's perspective. We have enough knowledge of God and glimpses of God's glory that we can have confidence in the everlasting God, the Creator of the ends of the earth.

To the everlasting God

Adoration

To the one who sits above the circle of the earth:
We offer thanks and praise.

To the one who stretches out the heavens like a curtain:
We offer thanks and praise.

To the one who spreads out a shelter for us to live in:
We offer thanks and praise.

To the one who can overturn the rulers and powers:
We offer thanks and praise.

To the one who calls us each by name:
We offer thanks and praise.

To the everlasting God, Creator of the earth:
We offer thanks and praise.

To the one who strengthens the powerless:
We offer thanks and praise.

To the one who helps us soar on wings like eagles:
We offer thanks and praise.

Creator God, accept our thanks and praise.
Amen.

You are the everlasting God

Confession

When I try to reduce you to a manageable size,
remind me that you are the Everlasting God:
The Creator of the ends of the earth.

When I have made of you something that suits my purpose,
remind me that you are the Everlasting God:
The Creator of the ends of the earth.

When I am led to despair by the state of the world,
remind me that you are the Everlasting God:
The Creator of the ends of the earth.

When I am too discouraged to stand up against evil,
remind me that you are the Everlasting God:
The Creator of the ends of the earth.

When I have been too busy, noisy
or self-satisfied to hear you call my name,
remind me that you are the Everlasting God:
The Creator of the ends of the earth.

When I have tried to do everything alone and in my own strength,
remind me that you are the Everlasting God:
The Creator of the ends of the earth.

For these and all the times when I have missed your way of love,
accept my confession and give me the strength to do better in the future.

Silence

Know that God will renew your strength and forgives your sins.
Thanks be to God.
Amen.

Imagining intercessions

Imagine that you are in space; picture swirls of stars, planets and great expanses of space. Imagine that you can see the Earth from a distance. See its atmosphere, the blues and greens of land and sea, the white bands of cloud. Notice the ice caps, mountains, oceans and deserts.

Silence

Creator God, we see in our mind's eye all that you have made. The heavens stretched out like an organza curtain glistening with stars. We see this planet, teeming with life, rich with possibility.

Yet we also see that the deserts have grown larger, the forests smaller. We know that the ice caps are melting and that pollution and human habits are damaging your world. We pray for our home, this place you spread out for us to live in; we remember people and creatures struggling to survive because of our misuse of your gifts.

Creator God, hear us:
Graciously hear us.

Imagine that you are walking along a rough road in Africa. You feel the warmth of the sun; see a wide expanse of grassland stretched out as far as the eye can see. The landscape shimmers in the heat haze. You think of the town you have just left, full of colour, sound, shouting, singing and laughter. A sophisticated town with a complex economy and wonderful history. Now the scene changes: people and trucks come towards you, carts laden with pots, pans, furniture, children and old people. Women are walking with huge packs on their heads and young men carry guns. Every so often a shout goes up, the convoy breaks into a run and you feel fear. The day becomes one full of refugees, talk of killings and famine.

Silence

Creator God, in our mind's eye we see familiar pictures, images that we have seen too often on our television screens. We see an African nation struggle; dignified women, children and men seek shelter and food. We too easily think that this is all there is to Africa, forgetting her rich history and her many contributions to the culture and commerce of the world.

We pray today for those places of famine, fear and starvation. Help us not to become immune to the horrors of war and poverty. We offer to you those who need urgent care today and pray that we will find ways to help build a fairer world for the future.

Creator God, hear us:
Graciously hear us.

33

Imagine that you are walking in the streets around this church. Who do you bump into? What shops and houses do you see? What sounds do you hear and what can you smell? Who do you talk with, and who do you walk past hardly noticing?

Silence

Creator God, in our mind's eye we see our neighbourhood and our neighbours. We know the issues and challenges for people who live around here – they are our issues and challenges too. In silence we name those people and those situations that need our prayers at this time.

Silence

We ask that you hold these people and needs close to your heart. Help us to respond as loving disciples, offering comfort, care and practical help; and teach us to love our neighbours as ourselves.

Creator God, hear us:
Graciously hear us.

Imagine that you are looking in the mirror! Look at the colour and shape of your eyes, the curve of your lips, the position of your hairline and your ears. Remember that God made you. Yes, really! God knows your name and calls you. Think of your likes and dislikes, your hopes and fears, the things you enjoy and the people you love. Remember that these are part of the 'you' that God is calling by name.

Silence

Creator God, in our mind's eye we see ourselves. We do not see as you see, and we do not always find it easy to value who we are. We think about our worries, our fears, and the people we care about, and sometimes we can feel unequal to the task of being your disciples. We grow tired, weary and disillusioned.

We pray today for those we love, silently naming those we have a particular care for at this time.

Silence

We pray for ourselves. Help us to hold on to the hope and confidence of our faith in you. Give us the courage and strength to live as your disciples in the world.

Creator God, hear us:
Graciously hear us.

Amen.

We have heard

Affirmation

Have you not heard?
It is God who stretches out the heavens like a curtain,
and spreads them like a tent to live in:
We have heard and we believe in God, our Creator.

Have you not heard?
It is God who has no equal,
who loves you, saves you and calls you by name:
We have heard and we believe in God, our Redeemer.

Have you not heard?
It is God who is the everlasting God, who grows not weary,
whose Spirit strengthens and upholds you:
We have heard and we believe in God, our Sustainer.

Amen.

May you rise

Blessing

May you rise up on wings like eagles.
May you run and not be weary.
May you walk and not be faint.
And may the blessing of the everlasting God,
Creator, Redeemer, Sustainer,
remain with you always.

Amen.

Worship setting ideas

Use lengths of material to represent God spreading the heavens like a curtain – deepest blue with tiny stars. Arrange images or globes of the Earth among the cloths, and candles.

Project on to a screen images of soaring eagles, or have images available to pass round during the service. Other images might be of people, young and old, running and laughing and playing.

During the intercessions, display images such as the following to help with the imagining:

> the planet – beautiful and damaged
> Africa – positive and negative
> your local neighbourhood – its good and bad news stories
> people's faces.

Action ideas

Get involved with campaigns against poverty, e.g. Comic Relief (see page 143).

Write to your Member of Parliament to protest against policies that maintain conflict in other parts of the world.

Campaign against the arms trade. It might be useful to get hold of a copy of *Peacemaking: A Christian Vocation*, available from MPH (see page 144), to find out how you and your church might contribute to peace.

Contemplating lofty aims

I want to mount up on wings like eagles,
only I need to get to the supermarket.

This is the problem with the sublime:
Life tends to be more about the mundane,
and I find I increasingly have little time,
to spend contemplating such aims.

I believe I can float on thermals with the breeze in my feathers,
but I'll be late for work if I don't go now.

I'm a feet on the ground kind of believer,
pragmatic, sensible, sane,
not easily led by a crafty deceiver,
who says I can fly with no plane!

I'd love to soar on the wings of God's love,
it's just that I've got to get the car serviced.

To be honest, it's not just the timing
that lowers my heavenly sights,
it's not even a doubt versus faith thing.
It's more that I'm frightened of heights!

Our heavenly Father

Teach us to pray

The Lord's Prayer, Matthew 6.9–15

Our heavenly Father,
like a Mother and a Father you love us unconditionally.
We worship your name,
you are holy and worthy of all our praise.
Your kingdom come,
your realm of love, peace and wisdom be real, here and now.
Your will be done, on earth as it is in heaven,
help your children in the way of obedience, that creation will be restored.
Give us today our daily bread,
grant us food for our bodies, your word for our spirits
and your Son's body and blood for our growth in grace.
Forgive us our wrongdoing,
your generous grace is more than we deserve.
As we forgive those who have wronged us,
help us to reflect your mercy and to love our enemies.
Do not bring us to a time of trial,
and protect those we love.
Rescue us from evil,
help us to fight for justice and good in the world.

Amen.

A word that carries so much

Reflection

In its many forms, settings and interpretations, the Lord's Prayer leaves us in little doubt that Jesus addressed God as 'Father'. Here is one of the linchpins of trinitarian theology. Father, Son and Holy Spirit. Such an address is personal and intimate, indicating a quality of relationship that is based on love, knowledge and respect.

Every word we use to describe or address God is laden with meaning. Many people find the term 'Father' problematic. For some this is a general resistance to using only male terms to refer to God. This patriarchal bias in language should not be too difficult to overcome in free churches where we can choose the metaphors, titles and names with which we refer to God. We can explore female imagery for God, 'a mother hen', for instance. Biblical material and historical precedents support this approach. It helps if we recognize that all our language about God is provisional (based on partial knowledge) and metaphorical because human language cannot hope to describe the divine creator of all that was, is and ever shall be.

The word 'Father' itself carries both positive and negative meanings for different people. Those who have suffered abandonment, abuse or cruelty at the hands of their father find the word difficult to hear with the frequency it is used in church. It is not sufficient to offer simplistic comfort such as 'we are referring to a perfect heavenly Father'. The word carries too much pain to be objectified in this way. For others, though, 'Father' is a word that carries memories of love, acceptance, kindness, tolerance and loving nurture.

It would be difficult to celebrate and explore the Trinity without visiting the traditional three-fold formula, Father, Son and Holy Spirit. Most of this book offers different metaphors, but here we pause to consider God as Father.

Prayer that struggles to find the right words

I do not want to call you 'Father' God.
I find it so hard to say that word with any helpful feeling.
Do you care if I address you with words that I refuse to imbue with meaning?

We glibly address you in forms that foster old orders,
ancient untruths about men,
while women remain invisible in our liturgy.

God, do you really want to be called King, Powerful Lord?
Just look at what the kings, the powerful lords have done to your world,
to your people, to your story!

Does it offend you that we choose limited language,
metaphors that marginalize and acronyms that support abuse?
Surely these concerns are more than postmodern sensitivities?

Shall we choose our words more carefully,
or stop using words altogether, seeking to be in your presence,
silently waiting for you to give us new words?

Hear the pain of those who can no longer pray;
heal the wounds of careless language and limited imagination;
hold the unspoken words of pain, passion and praise
until all your people can say 'Amen'.

My children's father

Poem

Tall, strong, gentle man,
I watch you from across the room
as you hold our son.
He fits between your elbow and hand,
balanced in complete security.

You and he are in your own world,
in this moment only the two of you exist.
All of love, all of God
fills you and flows from you;
balance returns to the universe.

Your eyes are linked by an invisible force
and with indulgent, passionate love
you are one, yet more,
greater than the sum of your parts,
balanced in a perfect moment.

Patient carpenter, you shape
wood, choosing colour, grain, heart.
Teaching our daughter
the names of the tools, as she sits
balanced on your knee.

You are both absorbed, intense
concentration, caught up in the act
of creation and recreation.
Her delightful giggle and your deep laughter
balance in harmony.

Your whole being is engaged
with the task and privilege of fatherhood.
Lifetime bonds being forged,
honed and grown, bringing to our home
balance and delight.

43

In love's embrace

A reflection on Rembrandt's painting 'The Return of the Prodigal Son'

I feel the weary weight of your arms
     as you embrace me
and the weary wait of your years
     of grief and loss.

You who were father and mother to me
     have no reason now
to offer open-handed welcome
     when I have deeply wounded you.

I can only bring a wasted, hollow shell
     of who I was, a shadow
of your hopes and dreams, your child
     who followed an empty vision.

Yet your welcome is overwhelming
     far beyond my dark imagining.
Your passion and generosity
     flow in tears and gifts, too real.

There is jealousy here, a quiet cynicism
     and a surly envy.
Those who doubt me know me well
     and question the wisdom of welcome.

I too doubt myself, can I live this life?
     But, here in love's embrace,
is the seed of grace, the heart of hope
     and the beginning of a new journey.

(Previously printed in the Methodist Prayer Handbook 2006/07)

Shapers of love

Thanksgiving and intercession

Mother, Father, God,
loving parent,
patient shaper of all creation,
nurturer of all creatures, lover of all people.

Thank you for parents,
giving freely of their time, love and experience,
shaping a new generation,
offering themselves in the all-consuming challenge of parenthood.

Give energy and courage to all those who bring up children:
mothers, fathers, grandparents, foster carers, guardians and care agencies.
Give wisdom to those who shape the future by loving today.

We pray for those who find caring for children a struggle:
mothers with post-natal depression,
parents whose children are ill or hard to care for,
fathers who feel excluded from family life.

We pray for those who remember their own childhoods with pain:
those for whom the words 'father' or 'mother'
bring memories of regret, hurt, injury, fear or anguish,
those who remember only abuse, neglect, disapproval and anger.

We pray for those who choose to break the pattern of the past:
those who work hard to build safe and loving homes,
those who will not be chained to patterns of fear, abuse and regret,
those who say, 'Things will be better for my children.'

Mother, Father, God,
loving parent,
patient shaper of all creation,
nurturer of all creatures, lover of all people:
Hear our prayers.

Amen.

Bless the sleepless nights

Bless the sleepless nights, the early mornings,
the nappies, the crying, the weaning and loving.
Bless the perfect moments, the giggles, the smiles,
the bonds forged of love's ancient forces.
Bless the mums and dads, grannies and grandpas,
the extended family loving the chaos.
In the name of God,
mother, daughter, lover.

Amen.

Worship setting ideas

Images of the Madonna and Child, of Christ's nativity or pictures of family groups could all be used in a service that explores the parenthood of God. A very helpful resource is *Born Among Us*, a pack of nativity images and worship ideas from around the world, available from MPH and USPG (see page 144).

Celebrate those who have been 'parents in faith'. Suggest that people bring in an object that represents an important person in their childhood or faith journey, and ask them to talk about that person. Place the objects on to a worship focus at the front of the church.

Action ideas

Plan an act of worship focusing on the work of NCH (see page 144) or another children's charity. Have a special collection or fundraising event for the charity.

Celebrate grandparents in the church. Organize a reminiscence project, where children and young people interview older people. Put up an exhibition: display photos and objects showing things that matter to the different generations in your church; or, even better, in your wider community.

Set up a babysitting scheme to give stressed parents a break. (Make sure that those taking part in the scheme are properly checked under safeguarding policies.)

Daddy, my Daddy

It gets to me
every time I watch *The Railway Children*.
The adolescent girl runs along the platform,
she shouts, 'Daddy, my Daddy!'
crying out with love and longing for the brave and wise man
returning from unjust imprisonment.

It gets to me
every time,
most of all because
I wish I could ever have felt that way about my own father.

He died.
Kind people said,
'You must miss him dreadfully.'
I wish I did.

I do not mourn his passing, instead
I mourn how things might have been.

I wish he had known how to love.
The damaged boy grew up into an angry man who learnt that
the only way to deal with pain is to shout, hit and shout some more;
the only way to handle things that get too hard is to walk away;
the only way to cope with people who are different is to hate them.

My grief is not for a lost love,
a lost relationship,
a box full of memories.

My grief is that we did not share those things,
that we did not have love,
that we could not speak truth to each other.

My grief is that I feel so angry that he did not let go of the hurts of his sordid
childhood, that those who damaged him gave him no means of healing himself.

I wish I could cry, 'Daddy, my Daddy!'

Living
Water

Under her wings

A psalm of birthing

A new psalm

O Yahweh, God of all creation,
O Holy One, whose hands made the heavens and the earth,
I cried out to you in my distress,
I shouted in the dark hours of the night.

I laboured long and hard;
the effort overwhelmed me.
So small this effort in the face of your great deeds.
How hard were the labour pains that welcomed creation?

I cried hot tears and knew no rest,
weeping gave me no relief.
My lover's hands brought comfort to my fevered brow,
his voice gave me courage.

You, child, I have carried,
in the depths of my being I have held you.
Little one, we have shared each breath,
Hearts beating in complementary rhythms.

Harder I work, driven on by primeval forces,
labouring you into being.
Separation marks completion,
your breaths are your own.

O Yahweh, as you released your child into being,
O Holy One, as you took the risk each parent knows,
Did you understand the fear mixed with excitement?
Do you know the love mingled with the poignancy of parting?

I carry my child in new ways now,
my infant grows stronger each day.
I watch my child walk without me,
and labour continues for years beyond birth.

Praise God for each space pregnant with possibility.
Praise God for each word that changes the world.
Praise God for inspiring courageous love.
Praise Mother, Child and Holy Spirit.

The heart of Mother God

Reflection

Is there something more distant in the role of father than of mother? Not necessarily once the child is born and weaned, but before birth, from the moment of conception, the father's role is by necessity more hands off than that of the mother. When working with metaphors of the Trinity we connect 'Father' with the Creator who brought all things into being. This is the omnipotent, transcendent God, beyond all knowing, unreachable, who watches the world 'from a distance'. It is in the incarnation that human beings can begin to touch God – can grasp the intimate, immanent nature of divinity held in a woman's womb. The complete 'embodiment' of God become human was enfolded and held within Mary's body. The embryonic and foetal Jesus could have no physical existence beyond that space; all that was needed for existence was provided through the umbilical cord. Mary's breath, her life force, gave Jesus life. Each cleansing inward breath provided oxygen; her blood cells coursed through his veins; her heartbeat was the first sound that he heard.

We call this intimate, vulnerable human baby 'Christ', 'Messiah', 'the Word of God incarnate'. I wonder what baby names Mary called the divine manifestation of God as she nursed him on her knee? What nursery rhymes did Jesus learn? What were his chores around the home, and was he scolded when he forgot to do them?

We know very little about Jesus' childhood but we do know that in the midst of his ministry he refused to see his mother and family. Yet with his dying breath he asked his friend to ensure that Mary would be cared for. The incarnate God understood what it was to be loved and nurtured. A few days before his death he had appealed to Jerusalem from the very depths of maternal longing: 'How often have I desired to gather your children together as a hen gathers her brood under her wings, and you were not willing!' (Matthew 23.37).

The 'Word' of God is more than an idea, an abstract concept. The wholeness of God is only complete through the 'second' person of the Trinity – given life through the courageous involvement of a young woman.

Magnificat adoration

Luke 1.46–55

In our deepest being, we magnify God,
our spirits rejoice in God our Saviour.

God has looked with favour on the lowliness of his servant.
Surely, from now on, all generations will call me blessed:
for the Mighty One has done great things for me,
and holy is God's name.

In our deepest being, we magnify God,
our spirits rejoice in God our Saviour.

Those who worship God will be shown mercy,
from generation to generation.
God has shown strength,
scattering the proud in the thoughts of their hearts.

In our deepest being, we magnify God,
our spirits rejoice in God our Saviour.

God brings down the powerful from their thrones,
and lifts up the lowly.
God fills the hungry with good things,
and sends the rich empty away.

In our deepest being, we magnify God,
our spirits rejoice in God our Saviour.

God helps the people Israel,
and never forgets to be merciful.
God remembers the promise made to all people,
in every generation.

In our deepest being, we magnify God,
our spirits rejoice in God our Saviour.

God is waiting

Confession

As a mother cares for her children,
God cares for us.
We confess that at times we have taken that care for granted.
We have trusted in our own strength.
We have turned away from God's love.

In quietness we remember before God
the times when in thought, word and deed,
we have failed to reflect God's love to the world.

Silence

Even when we have travelled away from God's care,
God is waiting, ready to run and meet us,
with open arms of love and consolation.

Know in your hearts that your sins are forgiven.
Thanks be to God.
Amen.

For the dawning of light

Thanksgiving

For the conceiving of new life, new ideas
and the possibility of a new creation:
We give thanks.

For the gestating of new life, new ideas
and the reality of a new relationship:
We give thanks.

For the labouring of new life, new ideas
and the excitement of a new challenge:
We give thanks.

For the birthing of God's child, holy word
and the vulnerability of incarnation:
We give thanks.

For the delivering of God's child, holy word
and the dawning of light in darkness:
We give thanks.

For the crying of God's child, holy word
and the sound of redemption songs:
We give thanks.

For the presence of God's Spirit, holy dancer
and the music of transformation:
We give thanks.

For the fire of God's Spirit, holy dancer
and the burning call for justice:
We give thanks.

For the healing of God's Spirit, holy dancer
and the sanctification of creation:
We give thanks.

Lead us into life

Intercession

Confident of God's love, we offer our prayers for the world and its people.

God, you conceived creation in a moment of inspired and generous love.
Your life force has given this world beauty, energy and diversity.
Your passion has spread colour, sound and movement across the universe.

Your creation has been damaged by human ignorance and greed.
Your world suffers at the hands of the powerful and the needs of the powerless.
The colours of your universe are muted when we lack the passion to celebrate.

We pray for your world, for its polluted places and damaged environment,
that we will have the courage to create rather than destroy.

Creator God:
Lead us to life.

You created human beings in your likeness, male and female you created us.
You made us to live in relationship with one another and with you.
You will for us to live in peace and wholeness, loving justice and mercy.

Your people have turned away from the path of peace.
Nation fights nation and homes become a place of violence and fear.
The actions of your people are despised when we lack the vision to love.

We pray for your people, for those damaged by war, conflict and violence,
that we will have the courage to build loving communities.

Creator God:
Lead us to life.

You created your Church to be the body of Christ on earth.
You made her to be a place of warm and safe welcome.
You long for her to be united, offering mission and service in your world.

Your children have divided the body of Christ.
We have feared change and closed our doors to vulnerable people.
The motives of your Church are distrusted when we lack the courage of our convictions.

We pray for your Church, for her
halting attempts to make a difference in a complex world,
that we will have the courage to break down barriers.

Creator God:
Lead us to life.

In the name of Christ.
Amen.

We believe in God

Affirmation

We believe in God
whose love gave birth to all creation.

We believe in God
whose love was made known in a human child.

We believe in God
whose love was poured out as living Spirit.

We believe in God.
We believe in God.
We believe in God.

Amen.

Know that you are loved

Blessing

As a hen gathers her chicks beneath her wings,
so God longs to gather her children together.
Know that you are loved with the intimate love of the nursing Mother.
Know that you are saved with the passionate love of the caring Daughter.
Know that you are blessed with the inspiring love of the gentle Spirit.
Go in the peace of God.
Amen.

Worship setting ideas

Place a stone or wooden carving of a mother and child in a prominent place within your worship area. Someone in the congregation may have one; or they are widely available from craft and gift shops, some of those from Africa being particularly lovely.

Display around the church images of men and women in caring activities. Celebrate the role of women as mothers but also talk about the care offered by fathers and by women and men who are not parents.

Action ideas

Organize fundraising for your local maternity unit, for instance, if they are in need of specialist equipment. Or the money could enable the unit to provide items to make rooms comfortable for those who have suffered a stillbirth or late miscarriage.

Find out from your local social services department if it's possible to use your church premises as a contact centre for parents and children who can only see each other under supervised conditions.

How beautiful you are

I catch myself watching you
as you play in the garden,
bend in intense concentration over your latest craft activity,
mess up the kitchen making a sponge cake.
You look up and smile
but if you find I'm watching you too often
you ask what's wrong
and I tell you for the thousandth time that
I cannot believe how beautiful you are.

Amidst mud or glue, or clouds of flour
you giggle and grumble and grin your
way through life.

The distance between us grows
but so does the love.
Letting you grow up and be whole
is the hardest of all privileges.

I want to protect you,
to make everything perfect, precise, safe and sound.
I want to heal you, help you, hide you and guide you
but I do you no honour if I make the world
a saccharine place of empty security.

So live a real life, a full life,
a life with scratches and disappointments
that mark the truth of living in abundance.
Live a whole life, a generous life,
a life with ups and downs,
heartaches and joyful celebrations.
Live a human, glorious life,
and fly safe in the knowledge that I will love you
when the landings are smooth and
I will pick you up and love you still when the landings are rough.

Live a real life.

Drinking deep from the well

The encounter

John 4.7–26

Jesus: Good evening, sister, please give me a drink.

Woman: But sir, how is it that you, a Jewish man, ask a drink of me, a woman of Samaria? You will get us both into trouble!

Jesus: Don't worry, if you knew the gift of God, and who it is that is saying to you, 'Give me a drink', you would have asked me and I would have given you living water.

Woman: Ha! But sir, you have no bucket and the well is deep. Where do you get that living water? Are you greater than our ancestor Jacob, who gave us the well, and with his sons, his daughters and his flocks, drank from it?

Jesus: Everyone who drinks of this water will be thirsty again, but those who drink of the water that I will give will never be thirsty. The water that I will give will become in them a spring of water gushing up to eternal life.

Woman: Wow! Sir, give me this water, so that I may never be thirsty or have to keep coming here to draw water.

Jesus: Go, call your husband, and come back.

Woman: I have no husband.

Jesus: Quite right, for you have had five husbands and the man you are with now is not your husband. You are telling me the truth!

Woman: Sir, I see that you are a prophet! Perhaps you can answer a question of faith? Our ancestors worshipped on this mountain, but you Jews say that the place where people must worship is in Jerusalem.

Jesus: Woman, believe me, the hour is coming when you will worship God neither on this mountain nor in Jerusalem. You worship the unknown; we worship the known, for salvation will come from the Jews. But the hour is coming, and is now here, when those who understand what it is to worship will worship God in spirit and truth, for these are the ones God calls to worship. God is spirit, and those who worship God must worship in spirit and in truth.

Woman: I know that the Messiah is coming. When he comes he will proclaim all things to us.

Jesus: I am he, the one who is speaking to you.

The conversation

Reflection

It was in a coffee bar in a town-centre church in Lancashire. You could hear rain pounding on the flat roof above (never a good idea in East Lancashire, a flat roof!). There was nearly as much steam rising from the customers as from the boiler behind the counter. Hot cups of tea, coffee and chocolate were making the day slightly less miserable. Drinks cost less than a pound and it was one of the few places in town with room for a wheelchair or a pram.

Moira was just finishing her time on duty and decided to stay on for a well-earned coffee and cake before facing another wet wait at the bus-stop. She sat at the only space available, opposite a tired looking woman. They chatted about how dreadful the weather was, how the new leisure centre in town looked great but it was a shame the prices had gone up. Moira asked the woman her name, which was Christine. Christine told her that she really liked coming to the coffee bar because it was close to the hospital. Her young daughter was undergoing therapy for leukaemia and needed to be left to sleep. If her mum stayed with her, she would try and stay awake to talk, and that didn't do either of them any good. The church café was a Godsend, according to Christine; she could sit for a long time without being asked to move on. There are only so many times you can wander round a wet town centre without spending money. The coffee bar was more than a place to get a drink for Christine; she told Moira that she felt loved there, and it was a place of sanctuary and light in a time of need.

An ordinary, everyday conversation at a place of refreshment became something more profound. These encounters are less mundane than might be assumed at first glance – the pastoral and theological heart of each person is not as hidden as we might suppose. In the encounter between Jesus and the Samaritan woman we eavesdrop on a conversation that began with simple needs and ended up with the revelation of the Messiah. The conversation led to the restoration of relationships and the transformation of a whole community. Who knows where a simple chat might lead?

You come to us as living Word

Opening prayer

Loving God,
who comes to us as living Word:
Teach us to listen.

Loving God,
who is known to us in the other person:
Teach us to listen.

Loving God,
who is known to us as a still, small voice:
Teach us to listen.

Help us to choose our words carefully, and our silences wisely.
Make us more ready to listen than to speak,
to speak than to act, to act than to ignore injustice.
Amen.

Who am I in this story?

Reflection on John 4.1–42

Am I the man, weary from travelling, the weight of the world resting on shoulders that do not seem broad enough for expectations of Messiah?

I have worked hard, listened carefully to the hints and leadings of my God. I have looked for the glimpses of divine light and recognized in each sign, each miracle, each life turned around, something of who I am. It seems a long, long time ago since those early signs, the early affirmation of temple teaching, and a meeting with the baptizer. I have worked hard, showing a different kind of power, but the holy, righteous ones who move to hypocrisy's beat seem threatened by one not motivated by wealth or war.

So I have travelled here, taken a long way round to avoid the machinations of the mighty. I stand on foreign soil, yet this is holy ground, this is the well of my ancestors. Those who would see the people of this land as cursed so quickly forget that we share our parentage. All this conflict, prejudice and pointless prattle about purity – it makes me so very tired. So many people, so many demands, so much time wasted on things that are not important. So I will stop. I will rest. I will take this moment to be – perhaps for once it won't be me that has to make everything all right, to solve every problem, to keep the show on the road. I have worked so hard and here I am, dusty, weary, tired of travelling and not even a bucket to draw from the well. I am thirsty.

Am I the woman, boldly, expectantly approaching the well, sure to fill my jar brimful with clean water?

I walk with expectation, my head held high. Let them watch, let them stare – they think I am no better than I should be. I walk in the burning heat of the day, as they stay cautious, trapped behind old doors and old ways of being. They expect so little of life and so all their expectations are met. I was not prepared to be trapped by their laws, by their tut-tutting and traditional ways. I found love after many heartaches and they would destroy it to prevent their social insecurity. I have learnt about longing and hoping and expecting. I have cared for him in the heat of the day, this last man and only love. He is thirsty all the time, feverish, needing to be looked after. I make many trips to the well these days and return taking care that not one precious drop is spilled. In every trip to Jacob's well I carry hope that this water will heal my love; I walk with expectation. Water to wash, water to cook, water to rinse away the gossip and grime of their misjudgement.

I walk with expectation. I believe in God, in Yahweh, in something more than can be seen or understood. I walk with expectation.

Am I a villager, a person of good standing, I know how things should be, I know right from wrong?

It's not difficult; the way we should live is laid down in our holy books and taught by our priests. We are to worship on Mount Gerizim, to live according to the commandments of God handed down by the prophets and makers of the law. Of course, the Jews look down on us, make out that we are less pious, less holy than they are – as they build their temples bigger and watch the poor die in the streets. I'm not judgemental – oh no, no one's perfect, but wrongdoers should be dealt with through the full force of law. We have to be careful; there are powers, political and military, that we have to be wary of. So I keep my head down. Not like some, well, one that I could mention.

I know how things should be. If everyone took our scriptures seriously then our town wouldn't be in such a mess. All sorts of travellers are allowed in, people don't follow the food laws as strictly as they did in my day – and the young people! Aimless, listless lot, all they seem to want to do is have fun – well, if they read their scriptures they would know that parties always lead to trouble. I know how things should be.

Am I a disciple, devoted to Jesus and busy with the demands of ministry?

I'm tired of doing, doing, doing. I don't think he realizes how busy we all are – especially me (some of the others don't pull their weight, you know!). Food doesn't just appear, we have to go and buy it, or work for it. Beds have to be found for the night – this being on tour is just one long round of administration. I don't think this is what I signed on for.

When he called me I knew so deeply in my heart that I had to follow him. It was so amazing at first: I was enthusiastic, caught up with the wonderful things he had to say – they made sense, not just in my head but in my soul. And the miracles! Well, that certainly held my attention – all those crowds pressing in to see him, so many voices. There's nothing like 5,000 voices singing a psalm to recharge your batteries. But most days are not like that. Don't get me wrong, I still love him and I still want to do his work, but I'm tired of doing, doing, doing.

Now we're really under pressure – the authorities in the capital are turning up the heat. A lot of those who liked Jesus are keeping their distance – he's a bit too challenging for these modern times. So we're off on our travels again. We've got to go into town and check things out. I like it better when we're at Simon's house, or with Mary and Martha – sitting around telling jokes, with a woman to bring us food and wine. Sharing bread and wine with him is just the best – but, like I say, these things don't just happen. Someone's got to sort out the nitty-gritty and if I don't do it, I don't know who will. I'm so tired of doing, doing, doing.

The meeting place

Prayer for gathering

Creator God,
we gather at this well, this place of meeting,
speaking, laughter and tears.
Be with us in the encounter:
And open our hearts to your word.

Creator God,
we see through tired eyes the familiar, the mundane,
yet glimpse the possibility of extraordinary revelation.
Be with us in the encounter:
And open our hearts to your word.

Creator God,
we are thirsty, looking for refreshment,
anxious that we do not have the means to
draw from the depths of your love.
Be with us in the encounter:
And open our hearts to your word.

Amen.

He was special

Reflection

Something came over me, something irresistible! As we talked together I felt a warmth; it's hard to describe, but it was very real. My heart felt different – it was beating fast with excitement, but it also seemed larger, as though there was room enough to love the whole world! I knew what love was when I looked at him: not some poor copy of love, but the genuine article – a deep, profound inner certainty that everything was going to be all right.

I knew from the moment he first spoke that he was special. He didn't worry about the old rules – rules that keep men and women, Jew and Samaritan apart. He knew that the things that matter go deeper than all that. The things that matter are not about the outward person, but are about knowing that I am God's child, loved, healed, restored – even forgiven!

I loved being with him but I knew it would be selfish to keep him all to myself. I ran as fast as I could (almost knocked his disciples over in my rush) back to the village. I knocked on doors, shouted, sang and danced. I think they thought I was possessed – they don't normally pay me much attention, but they did that day. A crowd began to gather and I told them that he was the chosen one, the one we had waited for – the one that would save the whole world. His love wasn't just for the Jews, or just for the men, or just for the free – it was something that poured and gushed and sprang, like water, living water.

They must have seen that I had changed, that something wonderful had happened, because they all wanted to have a look. Perhaps some were convinced, others just curious, so they went to see for themselves.

Our town's never been the same since. Once people had met Jesus they didn't need to hear my story any more – they understood for themselves. We have a confidence now; oppression from the Romans and grumpy behaviour from our Jewish cousins doesn't really bother us much. We seem to have a courage that comes from loving each other and from knowing that God loves us.

We do have bad days – people fall out, crops fail and things don't all go to plan. But our lives are better. It's not that we are protected from bad things, more that we are better able to cope when bad things happen. I still go to the well in the middle of the day, just in case I see him again, though they say things didn't go well for him. I don't know about that, though – I still feel his presence. I also go to the well when the others are there and we laugh and cry together, tell our stories and then walk back to town together – sometimes we even sing God's praise.

Moving out

Prayer for parting

Generous God,
thank you for the living water that is offered by your Son.
Thank you for the chance to pause again at the well of your deep generosity,
to taste again the sweetness of your love.

Thank you for space and peace,
for beauty and friendship,
for acceptance and laughter.

Let us move from our encounter with you back to our communities,
refreshed and invigorated.
Grant us the courage and strength
to share your living water with those we meet
and to be part of the healing and renewing of all creation.

Amen.

Worship setting ideas

Choose a focal point in the room (in the centre of the group, or on a platform at the front). Place lengths of sandy or brown cloth over a low table and across the floor to represent the wilderness. On the table place a large bowl, out of which flow blue and green cloths – water flowing in the wilderness. Fill some low basins with water and place them at different levels and float leaves, petals or candles in them. On the wilderness cloth place driftwood, stones, prickly plants and suitable flowers. To the side of the 'water' have pebbles, shells and a net.

Action ideas

Find out about and fundraise for the charity WaterAid (see page 144). Or raise money for MRDF (the Methodist Relief and Development Fund) and ask them to use it for a water-based project.

Organize a car-cleaning session for people living near the church. Hand-washing cars with buckets uses a lot less water than hoses or drive-through car washes.

Ask everyone at church to put a 'hippo' (see page 143) or other water-saving device into their toilet cisterns.

Just an ordinary coffee shop

Balancing precariously,
poised and promising a particular kind of refreshment,
are the two cappuccinos and three lattes on my tray.

This is my well,
this the place of encounter, gossip, thirst-quenching
friendship and rippling laughter.

This is a wishing-well,
where good wishes are offered as an acceptable
cover for the 'I love you' that is deeply meant.

This is a communal well,
where chance encounters rub shoulders
with planned meetings and happy coincidences.

This is a being well,
not a place for doing, for actions and deadlines looming,
the space offers well-being in a crazy world.

This is no special well,
just an ordinary coffee shop, one of dozens in this town,
but in the encounter I am transformed.

This is a sacred well,
in the laughter, the tears, the sharing and departing,
the rituals of embodied human living are practised.

I make it safely to our table and
the predictable pattern begins; creamy foam licked from a spoon
and in the encounter with the apparently mundane
I meet the divine.

Living water, living word

A wake for Miriam

Numbers 20

Find water for drinking, water for washing, water for ritual cleansing.
Find the water, Miriam; use your divining powers.
Help your sisters to draw water, while your brothers pour out endless laws
    and cleanse us with Yahweh's word.

In the wilderness of Zin,
in the place called Kadesh,
you died, Miriam, and we grieved as we buried you.

Who will find the water to wash the grave soil from our hands?
Who will find the water to wash the pain from our hearts?
Who will find the water to keep us alive in this Godforsaken place?

Moses, with your laws and plans, what use are they if we die of thirst?
Moses, with your tablets of stone, will they feed us when our animals starve?
Moses, with your Yahweh yearning, take us back to the old familiar landscapes.

What kind of wake can we offer you, Miriam?
A funeral feast needs grain, figs, grapes and pomegranates.
In Egypt we would have said a proper prayer and sent you off in style.

Aaron, talk to Moses, get him to see sense.
Aaron, we are frightened, we are losing hope.
Aaron, stop hiding in your grief and rescue your people.

We watched you both go to the threshold of the holy tent.
We watched you fall on your knees, carrying all our despair.
We watched you wrestling with faith and doubt.

You led us to the rock, unyielding granite, hard like Edom's heart.
You led us to the glorious holiness of Yahweh, the one God.
You led us to living water, flowing over angry words, smoothing them to caresses.

We splashed in the spring, revelled in the ripples and drank deeply of love.
We danced in the sparkling jewels that form of light glancing on water.
We remembered Miriam and, in our dancing, grief was cleansed of anger.

In Kadesh, where Miriam died

Reflection

The Old Testament features many stories about God's people being in a wilderness and about the provident love of God saving their lives. This theme is not surprising, as a key event in the formation of the people of Israel is that of the Exodus, the 40 years of desert wandering before finding a new home. Within the experiences of journey and exile, time and again water is a symbol of God's providence. Even when the people doubt and rail against God, declaring they were better off as slaves in Egypt, God does not abandon them to death and thirst, but brings forth life-giving water.

It strikes me that we often miss an important detail in our reading of Numbers 20. At the very beginning of the passage it is stated that Miriam died and was buried. This simple statement is a bridge between the preceding passage that concentrates on the need for ritual cleansing with water, and the following story of there being no water.

Throughout history women have been the carriers of water; their hard labour has kept communities alive. Even now, millions of women walk each day, sometimes many miles, to carry water for food and for cleansing. Was Miriam the diviner for the children of Israel, able to find the sources of life-giving water? Her death marks the beginning of harsher times and a great deal of complaining. Perhaps she had been able to keep up the morale of the people, and in their grief at her death they stopped looking for the signs of life and water and began to look back to the 'good old days'. This is a natural grief reaction: depression, anger, nostalgia and an inability to get on with the ordinary, practical things of everyday living. So the people became thirsty – and dehydration does not make for good tempers and clear thinking.

Moses and Aaron would, we imagine, have been as grief-stricken as the people. They must certainly have been exhausted and very frustrated that the people were taking out their grief and anger on them and being thoroughly unreasonable. In their despair, Moses and Aaron turned to God, who provided all that was needed for life. Yet we also detect a note of judgement. God declared that Moses and Aaron will lead the people to the Promised Land, but not enter it, because they did not have faith that God's holiness would be shown.

The chapter began with Miriam's death and ends with Aaron's. It is as though a family is gathered, sharing the stories of their forebears, marking their history and drawing the map of their identity.

Your word sculpted water

Adoration

Generous God,
your word sculpted water, bringing forth land and life:
We adore you and worship you.

Your word inspired the people of Israel to risk the wilderness:
We adore you and worship you.

Your word moved Miriam to dance in praise of you:
We adore you and worship you.

Your word led Moses to find life-saving water for his people:
We adore you and worship you.

Your Word became flesh and offers us life-giving water:
We adore you and worship you.

Help us to be attentive to your word,
faithful in worship,
and generous in our living.
In Christ's name.
Amen.

Thirsting for forgiveness

Confession

When we have despaired, finding our pilgrimage dry and exhausting:
Forgive us.

When we have failed to see your abundant gifts before our eyes:
Forgive us.

When we have wished for old comforts rather than looking forward to new life:
Forgive us.

When we have missed our way and forgotten the focus of our faith:
Forgive us.

Help us to find again your providential way,
refresh us with your life-giving word,
cleanse us with the water of life.
Forgive us, in the name of Christ. Amen.

Know that your sins are forgiven,
walk in the confident knowledge of God's generous love
and live in the strength of the good news of Christ.
Amen.

Guide us through each wilderness

Intercession

God, whose Spirit drives your people out
from the comfortable, safe places,
guide us through each wilderness,
every tough and lifeless landscape
that would drain our energy and leave our souls parched.

Help us to find places of refreshment,
to wet our lips with your living water,
to drink deeply of your life-giving stream.

Help us to travel with our eyes open,
that we might glimpse your glory in unexpected places
and your presence in unlikely people.

Help us to remain attentive,
that we might see the wilderness as a place of beauty
and sanctuary that will bring us, in the end,
closer to the fullness of your grace.
In the name of the one tested in the wilderness.

Amen.

We walk boldly

Affirmation

In the wilderness, the challenging places of life:
We walk boldly, loved by God.

In the fertile pastures, the lands of plenty:
We walk boldly, loved by God.

At the margins, when outcast and exiled:
We walk boldly, loved by God.

In the centre, when accepted and honoured:
We walk boldly, loved by God.

In the school and in the prison cell:
We walk boldly, loved by God.

In the hospice and in the maternity unit:
We walk boldly, loved by God.

In the temple and the market-place:
We walk boldly, loved by God.

In our strength and in our weakness:
We walk boldly, loved by God.

Beauty in the bleakest landscape

Blessing

May God grant you the vision to see
    beauty in the bleakest landscape,
    truth in the most confusing of questions,
    glimpses of holiness in the darkness of despair.

May God,
    the Weaver of Life,
    the Author of the Word
    and the Source of all Wisdom,
bless you now and always.

Amen.

Worship setting ideas

Arrange three spaces in the centre of your worship area. One represents things in our past that we look back on with pleasure or nostalgia; one represents what we look forward to. The third represents now, this place and this time. Bring some objects and pictures that help you to illustrate these three aspects of your own story. Hand out sheets of paper and invite people to write or draw some of their good memories, what they look back on with nostalgia and place them (or have them collected) in the first space. Offer prayers of thanksgiving for these memories.

You could include an element of confession for those events or deeds in the past that are not so pleasant, that we find hard to let go of, that stop us from moving faithfully into the future.

Later in the worship, ask people to draw or write something that represents where they are now – particularly what concerns them in their own lives and in the world. Have these brought forward to the space, then offer a prayer of intercession.

As an act of faith and affirmation, invite everyone to do the exercise again, this time looking to the future. Offer a prayer of affirmation and faithful commitment to our future with God.

Action ideas

We know much about Moses and Aaron from the Bible but Miriam gets considerably less coverage. We can also be sure that many other women had significant parts to play in the life of the community. Today, around the world, women are often invisible in the realms of government, commerce and the places of power. Women make up the majority of farmers in the world and, like Miriam and the women of Israel, also the majority of refugees. Contact the Women's Network of the Methodist Church, the Mothers' Union, the Women's Institute or UNIFEM (see page 144) to find out about projects that enable, empower and encourage women and girls around the world today.

Of course, we don't know if Miriam was the water diviner in her community, but clearly when she was no longer with them the people of Israel were lost without her. List the tasks that need doing in order to keep your church going – include jobs held in high esteem and those taken for granted. Is there an imbalance between women and men, young and old? If so, does this matter? Is it something that needs to be responded to? You might also consider if anyone is doing more than his or her fair share. Are there people in your church family who have things to offer who are not enabled to take part?

Diviner's intervention

Apparently it's not just me
who sits in a meeting,
calmly suggests a cracking idea,
has it ignored,
only for a few minutes later
a bloke to say the self-same thing,
and everyone to say,
'Excellent! Great idea, let's do that.'

As the room clears
the voices fade, saying,
'He's a good chap, you can always rely on him to hit the nail on the head.'
I sit and wonder if invisibility is a gift or a curse.

I am the water diviner.
I am the finder of the solution.
I am the word in season,
the wisdom, not of Solomon,
but of Bathsheba, of Miriam, of Mary Magdalene.

Written out of history,
written out of the canon,
written out of minutes, and reports.
Unheard,
unrecognized,
unseen, yet somehow
undaunted.

Go and find your own water.
Go and find your own solution.
Go and find your own word of wisdom.
I am woman and I will write my own history.
I will write my own canon.
I will write my own account of the things that matter.

Ignore me at your own risk.

Making connections

God was with the boy

Genesis 16 and 21

Narrator: Sarai, Abram's wife, had no children. She had an Egyptian slave girl, Hagar.

Sarai: Abram, you see that Yahweh has not granted me children. Take my slave girl in my place; it may be that I shall obtain children by her.

Narrator: Abram listened to Sarai. So after ten years in the land of Canaan, Sarai took Hagar and gave her to her husband as a wife. Abram showed no reluctance about this arrangement. When Hagar saw that she had conceived she looked with contempt upon her mistress.

Sarai: Abram, may the wrong done to me be on you! I gave my slave girl to your embrace, and when she saw that she had conceived, she looked upon me with contempt. May Yahweh judge between you and me!

Abram: Your slave girl is in your power; do to her as you please.

Narrator: Sarai dealt harshly with Hagar, and she ran away from her. The angel of God found Hagar in the wilderness by the spring of water on the way to Shur.

Angel: Hagar, slave girl of Sarai, where have you come from, and where are you going?

Hagar: I am running away from my mistress, Sarai.

Angel: Return to your mistress, and submit to her. I will give you so many children that they cannot be counted.
Now you have conceived and shall bear a son, you shall call him Ishmael, for God has given heed to your distress. He shall be a wild ass of a man, ready to fight everyone, and they will be ready to fight him. He will live at odds with all his kin.

Hagar: You are El-roi, the God who sees. Have I really seen God and remained alive?

Narrator: Hagar called the well Beer-lahai-roi (the well of the living one who sees me). It lies between Kadesh and Bered. Hagar bore Abram a son; and Abram named his son Ishmael.
Abram was eighty-six years old when Hagar bore him Ishmael.
Abraham was a hundred years old when his son Isaac was born to him.

Sarah: God has brought laughter for me; everyone who hears will laugh with me. Who would ever have said to Abraham that Sarah would nurse children? Yet I have borne him a son in his old age.

Narrator: The boy Isaac grew. When he was weaned Abraham made a great feast but Sarah saw the son of Hagar the Egyptian playing with her son Isaac.

Sarah: Cast out this slave woman with her son; for the son of this slave woman shall not inherit along with my son Isaac.

Narrator: The matter was very distressing to Abraham on account of his son.

God: Do not be distressed, Abraham, because of the boy and because of your slave woman; do whatever Sarah tells you, for it is through Isaac that offspring shall be named after you. As for the son of the slave woman, I will make a nation of him also, because he is your offspring.

Narrator: Abraham rose early in the morning and gave bread and a skin of water to Hagar, putting it on her shoulder, along with the child. He sent her away. Hagar departed and wandered about in the wilderness of Beersheba.
When the water in the skin was finished, she placed the child under a bush, then went and sat down about the distance of a bowshot away.

Hagar: Do not let me look on the death of my child.

Narrator: She lifted up her voice and wept. God heard the voice of Ishmael; and the angel of God called to Hagar from heaven.

Angel: What troubles you, Hagar? Do not be afraid; for God has heard the voice of the boy where he is. Come, lift up the boy and hold him safe within your arms, for I will make a great nation of him.

Narrator: Then God opened Hagar's eyes and she saw a well of water. She went, and filled the skin with water, and gave the boy a drink.
God was with the boy. He grew up living in the wilderness and became an expert with the bow. He lived in the wilderness of Paran; and his mother found a wife for him from the land of Egypt.

How did we come to these times?

Reflection

How did we come to these times?
In Genesis, for goodness' sake, so early in the story, the seeds of hate were sown. Mother love mingled with jealousy. Brother love was prevented and the wisdom of old age became blinded by overweening ambition.

How did we come to these times?
Family feuds are always the slowest to heal, but several thousand years must be a record when it comes to bearing a grudge. We are so alike, each tribe, each wandering people, each creed. Every one of us is part of a limited story.

How did we come to these times?
When one army's budget is counted in trillions and arms' profits in billions, yet millions starve for the sake of pennies. When terror is seen as a separate issue from poverty; and those who died on one day in America matter more than 10 times the number who die of hunger every day.

How did we come to these times?
Are these things anything to do with us? What difference can we make? We have held our services of remembrance, stood in silence to pay due tribute to the past. Will we put as much effort into the future? If prejudice grows in our own hearts, how do we deal with it? Do we have hope that we will lift our eyes from despair and see a life-saving well before us?

How did we come to these times?
Will a new kind of nation be born that asks different questions? No longer, 'Where are you from?' but rather, 'What matters to you?' Not, 'What do you believe?' but, 'Who do you love?' Not, 'How much do you make?' but, 'What can I share with you?'

The Prince of Peace is waiting for his uncles to stop fighting, so that his children can know the fullness of life.

Blessed are the ones who work for peace

Litany

Voice 1:   We all bear grudges; it's human nature, isn't it?

Leader: Blessed are the ones who work for peace:
All: **They will be called children of God.**

Voice 1:   They're different – why should I care? They're nothing to do with me.

Leader: Blessed are the ones who work for peace:
All: **They will be called children of God.**

Voice 1:   But they're different – they worship in a different place, a different way.

Leader: Blessed are the ones who work for peace:
All: **They will be called children of God.**

Voice 1:   If we don't sell arms, someone else will. They might not be as careful as we are.

Leader: Blessed are the ones who work for peace:
All: **They will be called children of God.**

Voice 1:   If I shout louder and hit harder than the rest, my voice will be heard.

Leader: Blessed are the ones who work for peace:
All: **They will be called children of God.**

God have mercy

Confession

We see a world torn apart by hate.
Old wounds refuse to heal,
grudges continue from generation to generation.
God have mercy:
Christ have mercy.

We long for peace between nations.
Watching the unfolding horrors on our televisions,
we change channels because it's too much to bear.
God have mercy:
Christ have mercy.

We play our part in the conflicts of our time,
swapping a story at a friend's expense,
envying another's success.
God have mercy:
Christ have mercy.

We find it hard to live up to your teaching.
Forgiveness is a challenge for those
more worthy than we believe ourselves to be.
God have mercy:
Christ have mercy.

We struggle to find peace in our hearts,
filling the emptiness and fear
with those things that harm us and hurt others.
God have mercy:
Christ have mercy.

We long to meet the Prince of Peace.
Help us not to be satisfied with an absence of war
but to seek the peace that is offered by your Spirit.
God have mercy:
Christ have mercy.
Amen.

Thanksgiving for hints of peace

For each child who grows up knowing that they are loved.
Gracious God:
We give you thanks.

For each vulnerable child rescued from danger.
Gracious God:
We give you thanks.

For those who risk everything to protect a child.
Gracious God:
We give you thanks.

For each refugee who finds shelter and safety.
Gracious God:
We give you thanks.

For each asylum-seeker who is treated fairly.
Gracious God:
We give you thanks.

For every tiny inch forward towards peace in the Middle East.
Gracious God:
We give you thanks.

For every gun broken and weapon laid down.
Gracious God:
We give you thanks.

For your peace that is beyond our understanding.
Gracious God.
We give you thanks.
Amen.

We pray for peace

Intercession

Creation no longer groans in labour pains
but gasps in agony from the wounds of a thousand wars.
Human history bristles with battles
about birthright, land, water, religion and power.
It is easy to despair in the face of
humanity's apparent inability to live together.

God of love, we hold before you the places of conflict today,
praying that your Spirit of peace, joy and love
will restore creation and your people.

We remember every child who has been born
into conflict; whose toys are cast-off shell casings.
Prince of Peace:
We pray for peace.

We remember every victim of rape and torture
and each refugee running for his or her life.
Prince of Peace:
We pray for peace.

We remember each family in which conflict and abuse
are everyday realities.
Prince of Peace:
We pray for peace.

We remember those who have given up their lives
in the cause of peace.
Prince of Peace:
We pray for peace.

We remember those in power who choose between
war and peace, negotiation and military action.
Prince of Peace:
We pray for peace.

We remember that we can be bringers of peace
into our homes, our communities and our world.
Prince of Peace:
We pray for peace.
Amen.

We remember the peacemakers

Collect

Merciful God,
we remember before you the peacemakers in our world.

We pray for all who risk their own comfort
and safety in order to help make your world a safer,
more comfortable place for all.

We know that in every cruel act,
Christ is crucified again.
Yet in every act of self-sacrifice
we come face to face with the risen Lord.

Help us to be faithful risk-takers for the sake of love and peace,
joining, gracious God, in your work to renew creation.

If we are ever tempted to despair
or feel that the darkness will overwhelm us,
remind us that Christ is the Light of the World
and the darkness will never overcome that light.
In the name of the Prince of Peace.

Amen.

We are the peacemakers

Affirmation

We are the children of God,
sisters and brothers of Christ.
We live in the world that God has created.
Making peace is not someone else's responsibility:
We are the peacemakers.

We are the children of God,
people of the Word, a community of hope.
We live as the Body of Christ.
Making peace is not a job for the experts:
We are the peacemakers.

We are the children of God,
people united in mission and service.
We live inspired by God's Spirit of faith, hope and love.
Making peace is not for another day:
We are the peacemakers.

God of all Creation,
Prince of Peace,
Spirit of Hope,
We commit ourselves to work for peace, today and every day.
Amen.

Peace blessing

May God bless you and, in loving mercy, grant
peace in this world,
peace in this nation,
peace in your home
and peace in your heart.
In the name of the Prince of Peace.

Amen.

Worship setting ideas

Arrange a number of prayer stations around the room, some with images of conflict situations, others with symbols and images of peace. Include Bible texts about peace and conflict. Invite people to spend a time of prayer and reflection, moving around the prayer stations, offering thanksgiving and intercession as they feel led.

Give each worshipper a piece of paper in the shape of a dove (or with the outline of a dove printed on it). During the service ask them to write a situation in their life or in the world in which peace is needed. These can be collected and offered to God with one of the prayers above.

Lay out a large map of the world and invite people to place tea-lights on it to mark places of conflict that they wish to pray for.

Action ideas

Arrange a meeting at which leaders of the different faiths in your area can speak to your church members; or, even better, to the wider community in which you live. Create opportunities for spending social time with people of other faith communities.

Visit a local school to talk about peace, and teach the children to make origami 'peace cranes' (see page 144). Hundreds of thousands of these are made each year to commemorate Hiroshima and Nagasaki, destroyed by atomic bombs. They are a means of actively committing to a more peaceful world.

Raise money for local or national charities that offer refuge to those escaping domestic violence.

A fragile thread

Somewhere in the pattern of human history,
there is a strand of peace,
running like a fragile thread
through the tapestry of time.

It is said that in only one year in the twentieth century
was no British soldier killed in action.
What of all the soldiers and civilians
around the world who were killed that year?
In the face of despair do we give up on peace?

Two thousand years ago, in an occupied territory,
the Prince of Peace was born,
and children died.
Today that same territory is occupied,
and children die.
In the face of despair do we give up on peace?

To hope against hope
is what allows us to believe in resurrection.

Have we the hope needed to
live as people who believe that peace is possible
and to join God in weaving the fragile thread of peace
through the tapestry of time?

Light of the World

You are going to live

O God, I don't know

Ezekiel 37.1–14

The hand of God came upon me and led me out. God's Spirit set me down in the middle of a valley; it was full of churches. God led me all round them; there were very many lying in the valley, and they were very dry. God spoke to me, saying, 'Mortal, can these churches live?' I answered, 'O God, I don't know.'

Then God said to me, 'Prophesy to these churches and say to them: O dry churches, hear the word of God. Thus says God to these churches: I will cause my Spirit to enter you, and you shall live. I will give you a purpose and teach you to love, I will heal you and put my Spirit within you, and you shall live; and you shall know that I am God.'

So I prophesied as I had been commanded; and suddenly there was a noise, a rattling of keys and stone and windows, a clunking of pews and chairs, a breaking of glass. The churches came together, they found a purpose, but there was no life in them. God said to me, call to the Spirit; call, mortal, and say to the Spirit: 'Thus says God, come from the four winds, from the ends of the earth, breathe upon these dead churches, that they may live.' I prophesied as God had commanded me, and the Spirit came into them and they lived, they stood on their feet, a vast multitude.

Then God said to me, 'Mortal, these churches are the Body of Christ. They say, "Our churches are dried up, and our hope is lost, we are cut off and declining." Therefore prophesy, and say this to them. Thus says God, I am going to open your doors and bring you out from your buildings, and you are going to live. O my people, I will bring you back to life. You will know that I am God, when I open your doors and bring you out from your buildings, O my people. I will put my Spirit within you and you shall live, and I will bring you to a fertile place; then you will know that I, your God, have spoken and will act.'

Open your doors and live

Reflection

What are these dry churches that like dry old bones have withered and died? There is a great deal of talk in UK churches about decline: nostalgia for fuller churches and active young people's work, and fear that we can no longer 'keep the roof on'. For many this description is a sad and true reflection of their church experience. It is very painful to have found your identity, your partner, your purpose, even your salvation within a particular church community, only to watch it wither and be less than it once was.

There are also churches growing, with life and energy and vision. Here the Body of Christ is healthy and fruitful, sometimes in the hardest of soils – the places of real need for love. The apparently infertile soil of a very difficult housing estate in Swansea is the context for a church that looks outwards, welcoming children and young people to midweek activities; it has doubled its tiny Sunday congregation in two years. The Spirit's breath has blown here and people are finding new life.

The churches that can live again are those that look outwards, who open their doors, whose people go outside to encounter a world in need. The dry churches, the old bones, who can only look inwards, only protect that which is of a bygone age, these are the churches that will not live. Yet the Body of Christ will still flourish, and is growing where injustice is challenged, where hatred is not allowed to win, where relationships matter more than what kind of music is used in worship. The church communities that will contribute to the health of the Body of Christ are those where care is not restricted to those on a membership list, but who love each other and the world.

It is not only local churches that face these decisions; whole denominations do as well. Debates about leadership, structure and ecumenical unity are important, but if they are all that church structures offer, then they too will die. A prophetic voice is needed from the churches that will challenge injustice, offer a different perspective on the world and welcome the outcast and the stranger. Such a voice might raise the dead; it will certainly not be popular. Such a voice might also whisper an invitation to the Holy Spirit to renew and transform the Church.

A still point of grace

Prayer for gathering

Loving God,
We gather in this place of encounter,
each with our own needs, desires and concerns.

Some of us are here full of energy and anticipation,
open to new ideas, enthusiastic and affirmed in our discipleship.

Some of us are tired and weighed down,
like dry bones in a wilderness, not sure why we are here.

Some of us feel all these things at once!

So, gentle, healing and inspiring Spirit of God, accept us just as we are,
breathe your love and peace into our hearts, and let this time together
be a still point of grace in our busy lives.
In Christ's name.

Amen.

Spirit of God, we praise and adore you

Adoration

Spirit of God, you moved across the waters before all time began:
We praise and adore you.

Spirit of God, you breathed life into all living creatures:
We praise and adore you.

Spirit of God, you called Sarah and Abraham to travel an unknown road:
We praise and adore you.

Spirit of God, as cloud and fire you guided your people Israel:
We praise and adore you.

Spirit of God, you moved Miriam to dance:
We praise and adore you.

Spirit of God, you spoke through your prophet Ezekiel:
We praise and adore you.

Spirit of God, you led Jesus through the wilderness:
We praise and adore you.

Spirit of God, you gave birth to the Church at Pentecost:
We praise and adore you.

Spirit of God, you move in our lives and the Church today:
We praise and adore you.
Amen.

The restless movement of your Spirit

Confession

Generous, loving God,
we see glimpses of the glory of creation,
we know through Jesus the comfort of salvation,
we sense the restless movement of your Spirit,
yet we do not live as people of vision, knowledge and wisdom.

For the poverty of our worship:
Forgive us and renew your Spirit within us.

For our half-hearted attempts to live as your disciples:
Forgive us and renew your Spirit within us.

For those times when we have mistaken our church for a building:
Forgive us and renew your Spirit within us.

For those times when we have failed to love our neighbours as ourselves:
Forgive us and renew your Spirit within us.

In silence we offer our personal confession.

Silence

The Spirit of God lives to set us free.
Know that through Christ your sins are forgiven.
Be inspired by God's Spirit to live as children of God.
Amen.

Shouted, whispered and unspoken

Intercession

God of wisdom, as your prophets of old saw unlimited possibilities and called people to faithful living, grant us the vision needed to change your world.

Where the voices of greed drown out the voices of the needy,
where children die through malnutrition,
where countries are devastated by AIDS,
grant us the courage to make a difference, and:
Send your Spirit to bring new life.

Where the shouts of despair drown out the whispers of the hopeful,
where peace appears to be an unobtainable dream,
where well-being is measured in how much we own,
grant us the courage to make a difference, and:
Send your Spirit to bring new life.

Where the laughter of the arrogant drowns out the whispers of the broken-hearted,
where depressed people find only stigma and rejection,
where refugees are unwelcome and uncared for,
grant us the courage to make a difference, and:
Send your Spirit to bring new life.

Where the alleluias of the self-righteous drown out the prayers of the faithful,
where churches are dying through lack of vision,
where people of faith distrust each other,
grant us the courage to make a difference, and:
Send your Spirit to bring new life.

Hear all our prayers, shouted, whispered and unspoken.
Amen.

Do you believe in God?

Affirmation

Do you believe in God the Creator
who set your bones in place?
We believe in God the Creator!

Do you believe in God the Redeemer
who overcame death so all can live?
We believe in God the Redeemer!

Do you believe in God the Sustainer
who calls you from the wilderness to be God's people?
We believe in God the Sustainer!

Physical blessing

Feel God's blessing in your bones.
Sense God's blessing in your sinews.
Know God's blessing in your hearts.
Grow as the people God created you to be,
witness to Christ's love in the world,
and live inspired by the breath of the Spirit.

Amen.

Worship setting ideas

Use sand or pieces of cloth to represent a wilderness. Place cut-out paper bones on the cloth, along with a staff to represent the prophet Ezekiel.

During the reading of 'O God, I don't know', show OHP or PowerPoint® images of ruined and boarded-up churches. As the reading continues, show active churches engaged in community work – cafés, fairtrade stalls, parent and toddlers, etc. Ask your congregation which category your church belongs to – if you dare!

Action ideas

Find out about churches with interesting community work or mission projects. Arrange to visit one or two in contexts similar to your own. Are there things you can learn and introduce in your own church?

Contact your District Mission Enabler or Diocesan Evangelist (or equivalent) and invite her or him to share ideas with you about ways you might focus on mission in your area.

Have a church reflection day. Questions to ask might include:

Are we a church that is alive, or are we dry bones in the wilderness?

What is our 'wilderness' – what is our context?

What do we need to do to make our church live?

Who can we ask to share in making this happen? e.g. ecumenical partners, community groups, local council, mission enabler, etc.

Holy ground with splinters

I feel my energy drain away
as I walk apprehensively through the door,
my ambivalence and anxiety
causing interference with my good intentions.

Why have I come here?
This holy ground would give me splinters if I removed my shoes,
the paint peels mournfully on the walls
and the notices on the board are all at least six months past being useful.

Then the muttering begins.
'They've moved the chairs.'
'Don't like this new hymn book.'
'Who's that over there? Never seen him before –
he's sitting in Hetty's pew, that'll never do.'

If I wasn't preaching here today
I'd walk away.
I'd never darken this dark door again.
Into this atmosphere
of dank, dusty, lukewarm piety
I am called to bring good news –
Good News with a capital G and a capital N.

O God, breathe your Spirit into my
disheartened heart.
Inspire me to offer something that in this hour
will raise the dead.

Help me to offer a spark of life and light.
Breathe on these dry old bones,
live through these carefully chosen words
and lead me not into despair.

Remind me that this is the day of resurrection
and as I look with love and exasperation upon these your people,
remind me that with you anything is possible.

I will pour out my Spirit

Wonders and signs

Acts 2.1-21

It was the day of the festival of Pentecost. Jesus' followers were sitting together in one room, wondering what would happen next.

Without warning, a sound like the blowing of a violent wind came from heaven and filled the whole house. As the friends of Jesus looked around in astonishment they saw tongues of flame that separated and came to rest on each of them. Each person was filled with God's Holy Spirit and began to speak in other languages as the Spirit enabled them.

In Jerusalem faithful Jews from all over the known world were gathered for the festival. When they heard the sound of the wind and the voices of the disciples, a crowd gathered, bewildered because each could hear someone speaking in their own language.

In utter amazement people asked, 'Surely these people speaking are from Galilee? How is it that we can hear them speak in our own language? Parthians, Medes, Elamites, residents of Mesopotamia, Judaea and Cappadocia, Pontus and Asia, Phrygia and Pamphylia, Egypt and the parts of Libya near Cyrene, visitors from Rome, Cretans and Arabs – we hear them declaring the wonders of God in our own language!'

Amazed and perplexed, they asked one another, 'What does this mean?'

Some of the crowd made fun of the disciples, suggesting that they had drunk too much wine.

Peter stood up with the other disciples and spoke to the crowd. 'All of you, listen. Let me explain this to you. These people are not drunk. After all, it's only nine in the morning! Surely you are faithful Jews who know the words of the prophet Joel and see them fulfilled today?

"In the last days, God declares,
I will pour out my Spirit on all people.
Your sons and daughters will prophesy,
your young men will see visions, your old men will dream dreams.
Even on my servants, both men and women,
I will pour out my Spirit, and they will prophesy.
I will show wonders in the heaven above and signs on the earth below,
blood and fire and billows of smoke.
The sun will turn dark and the moon turn blood red
before the great and glorious day of God.
Everyone who calls on God's name will be saved." '

A new language?

Reflection

It is not easy to imagine ourselves in the disciples' shoes. Some weeks previously Jesus had been killed in a horrific and violent way. Since then he had appeared to them in a number of places, very much alive, engaged with the daily matters of fishing, walking and breaking bread. Did his leaving from each visit plunge them into the despair of bereavement again? All this coming and going must have been hard to take – not knowing if they would see him again. Then, a few days before the festival of Pentecost, Jesus made the most dramatic departure of all. He ascended into heaven before their eyes, having told them to stay in Jerusalem and wait for the gift of the Holy Spirit.

I wonder how sceptical the disciples were at this point? They must have been thrilled to have had so much time with Jesus after the crucifixion but there must also have been a constant anxiety about how long he would be with them. Were they angry or confused, frightened or calmly expectant? We can only imagine.

At Pentecost they gathered in a city full of orthodox pilgrims, just the sort of people to find Jesus' radical teaching hard to swallow. They huddled together in a room as the crowds milled around outside. There is nothing in the Bible text to help us understand the state of mind of the disciples at this time – perhaps they were hiding, or perhaps waiting in faithful expectation for the gift that Jesus had promised so often before.

Into this situation God poured the Holy Spirit. The disciples were transformed and nothing would ever be the same again. These followers of Jesus were given a new confidence to speak his word, even in languages they did not know. From despair and confusion was born a new movement, the Church of Christ on earth. The Spirit opened the mouths but also the hearts and minds of Christ's followers and a chain reaction began that continues to this day.

We modern western Christians may be able to relate to the disciples' experience of confusion and disconnectedness from the context we live in. It is easy to feel that we are under siege and need to hide from the world. The world does not see us as drunk, more likely mad or irrelevant. Surely, as inheritors of the same Spirit as those first believers, we can find a language to relate to the world around us? We can continue to overturn Babel with all its chaos by learning to speak in words that touch people and are relevant to their lives. The liberating mission of Christ to bring good news to the poor and to free the oppressed is as vital today as ever. Are we open to the Holy Spirit's movement of freedom and communication? Can we change the world?

We wait for you, Spirit of God

Prayer of approach

Spirit of God,
breathing, blazing, blessing,
inspire our worship,
ignite our passion,
inform our action.
We wait for you, Spirit of God.

Spirit of God,
dancing, delighting, descending,
move through our lives,
melt our hearts,
motivate our loving.
We wait for you, Spirit of God.

Spirit of God,
opening, offering, outpouring.
reveal truth to us,
renew our faith,
refine our discipleship.
We wait for you, Spirit of God.

Pentecost confession

We have ignored the prompting of your Spirit, urging us to act for justice and peace:
Forgive us and renew your Spirit within us.

We have used words as barriers instead of simply telling the story of your love:
Forgive us and renew your Spirit within us.

We have scorned those whose religious experience differs from our own:
Forgive us and renew your Spirit within us.

We have missed opportunities to talk about our faith and proclaim your word:
Forgive us and renew your Spirit within us.

We have hurt others, neglected our discipleship and lost our way:
Forgive us and renew your Spirit within us.

The Spirit of God is present with us now,
reminding us of Christ's promise that when we confess our sins to God,
we will be forgiven.

Know that you are forgiven.
In the name of Christ.
Amen.

Diverse and complex

Intercession

Spirit of God, your will is to draw people ever closer in community with you and with each other. In our prayers we remember places and people divided by circumstance, prejudice, misunderstanding and fear.

We remember creation, made diverse and complex, systems of life in fragile balance.

We recognize the damage caused by human greed, by ignorance of the consequences of our actions and by our inability to read the signs of decay.

We pray for . . .
(current issues of the environment and pollution)

Silence

Spirit of God:
Hear our prayer.

We remember humanity, made diverse and complex, designed to live as communities.

We recognize division and brokenness between nations, communities and individuals. We see the consequences of war, conflict, greed and hatred.

We pray for . . .
(current areas of war and conflict)

We remember . . .
Refugees and asylum seekers . . .
Victims of racism, homophobia, and prejudice of all kinds . . .

We pray for families and relationships that struggle to stay together or in touch, remembering . . .
Victims of domestic violence and abuse . . .
Children who long for safe homes . . .

Silence

Spirit of God:
Hear our prayer.

We remember the Body of Christ, made diverse and complex, called into being by the Holy Spirit.

We recognize the disunity in the Church, where the words we use and the traditions we live by seem to matter more than the quality of our relationships. We see the consequences of our unwillingness to listen to and learn from each other.

We pray for the Body of Christ throughout the world.

We remember our local Churches Together groups and our own efforts towards unity.

We pray that we will be open to your Spirit of unity, so that Christ's love might be recognized in the way that we love one another, within this church and within the wider family of God.

Silence

Spirit of God:
Hear our prayer.
Amen.

We know God's Spirit is with us

Affirmation

Before time began the Spirit of God hovered over the waters of creation:
We know God's Spirit is with us.

Throughout history, the Wisdom of God has woven the pattern of our humanity:
We know God's Spirit is with us.

At the turning point of God's salvation story,
Jesus Christ was filled with the Holy Spirit:
We know God's Spirit is with us.

When all seemed lost and abandoned, the Spirit danced as living flame:
We know God's Spirit is with us.

Today, in the Church and in the world, the Spirit continues the work of creation:
We know God's Spirit is with us.

In a future unknown but safe in God's hands, the Spirit moves in love's embrace:
We know God's Spirit is with us.
Amen.

Spirit blessing

Sense the warm passion of the Spirit's flame.
Speak with the fervour of the Spirit's voice.
Move with the music of the Spirit's dance.
May God's Spirit bless you, inspire you and confirm you
in your calling as a disciple of Christ.

Amen.

Worship setting ideas

Have long lengths of red and yellow cloth tucked into a basket, box or other container. As the Acts 2 passage is read, people can unfurl the cloths and spread them out, across the front of the church or right into the congregation. This is something that children present might enjoy helping with.

If your church has a one-line 'mission statement', or a favourite Bible text, create banners showing the statement in various different languages. Simple stencils of letters can be applied to lengths of silk or calico and then fabric paints used. If these are good enough you might want to have them displayed in church for some time.

Action ideas

Find out about the languages that are spoken in your church or wider community. Are there people who struggle with English? Can you offer English lessons to people in your community?

Do you use language in church that other people might find hard to understand? Think about how accessible your church is in terms of the words you use, but also in terms of your habits and your premises. Perhaps invite someone with no church background to spend time in your worship so they can share with you what it feels like.

Organize a church family day – away or on your premises – to share the dreams and visions of people of all ages in your church. What are the hopes of your young, middle-aged and older people? How can you work together to make them happen? When you share and talk together you might be surprised by how much you have in common, and by new and wonderful ideas that may emerge. Explore not only ideas for your church life but also how you might make faith relevant and accessible beyond your church.

A colour catches my eye

Lost in the hot crush of a heaving crowd,
I find myself frustrated by the tourist pace of casual, slow enquiry.
I am in a hurry.

I want to walk faster than this,
but the busy streets close around me.
I have a train to catch.

In the hustle of the holiday throng,
with a dozen languages
rough on my ears,
I stand still.

Between the buildings a colour catches my eye.
A banner of flaming red,
scorched with yellow,
burns for a split second.

Brought to my ears
on an impudent breeze,
the sound of a samba band
beating a rhythm of thunder and power.

From deep within my closed and worried throat
comes laughter,
uncalled for and unexpected,
bubbling up, brilliant with giggling joy.

I see myself lifted from sombre sobriety
to a state of intoxicated glee
that gives me a voice
and opens my eyes
to the reality of a city that is carnival chaos,
Mardi Gras magic and festival frenzied.

In a moment of grace
I know a new spirit,
moving my feet to a different rhythm
and my heart to a fuller way of loving.

121

The Spirit of God is upon me

The Spirit of God is upon me

Luke 4.14–30

Narrator: After Jesus had spent 40 days in the wilderness he returned to Galilee filled with the power of the Holy Spirit. People in the area heard wonderful reports of his preaching and he was invited to speak in their synagogues.

When he came to his home town of Nazareth, he went to the synagogue on the Sabbath day, as was his custom. He stood up to read and was given the scroll of the prophet Isaiah. He read the following words:

Jesus: The Spirit of God us upon me,
God has anointed me to bring good news to the poor.
I have been sent to proclaim release to prisoners,
recovery of sight to the blind,
to let the oppressed go free,
and to proclaim that this is the year of God's favour.

Narrator: Jesus rolled up the scroll, gave it back to the attendant and returned to his seat. The eyes of every person in the synagogue were fixed upon him as he said to them:

Jesus: Today this scripture has been fulfilled in your hearing.

Worshipper 1: He spoke so well and with such a lovely gracious voice.

Worshipper 2: But surely this is Joseph the carpenter's son?

Jesus:	I know what you are thinking. I dare say you will quote to me the proverb, 'Doctor, cure yourself!' and demand that I do in this my home town the things that you heard I did in Capernaum. Truly I tell you, a prophet is not accepted in the prophet's home town. Indeed, there were many widows in Israel in the time of Elijah, when there was no rain for three and a half years. You remember the story of how a great famine lay upon that land? Yet it was to a widow at Zarephath in Sidon that Elijah was sent. You also know that there were many lepers in the land of Israel in the time of Elisha, and none of them was cleansed except Naaman the Syrian.
Narrator:	When they heard this, all in the synagogue were filled with rage. They got up and drove Jesus out of the town, leading him to the brow of a hill so that they might hurl him off the cliff. But he passed through the midst of them and went on his way.

Not in your own town

Reflection

Things seemed to be going well. At the beginning of Jesus' public ministry he gained a great reputation. Filled with the Holy Spirit, his preaching was very popular and people began to invite Jesus to speak in their synagogues. During this fruitful time he went home to Nazareth where he had been brought up. Being a devout and observant person of faith, he attended the synagogue on the Sabbath.

I remember going back to my home church some years after leaving. I was asked to read the Gospel as part of an anniversary service. It was a strange experience, so much was familiar and yet some things had changed. The building had been refurbished to a high standard, with some interesting colour choices. I imagined the conversations that had taken place over that decision! I recognized many of the people there; a few faces were missing because faithful people had died and a few families had moved away. The strangest thing of all was how much I had changed and how I could not begin to explain that to those who had stayed. My life was different now, with new friends and experiences. My point of view had altered and part of me wanted to share that with friends in my old church family. But for most people there I was still a young teenager, with little experience; they knew me as who I had been then and not who I am now. Unlike Jesus, I did not expand on the word that I read, which may have been a blessing for all!

Jesus' perspective had changed since being a child in Nazareth; he had broadened his horizons and struggled with his own sense of calling to a difficult ministry. As he was invited to read from the scroll I wonder what motivated him to choose that passage. Luke 4.18–19 is often called Luke's 'manifesto' – it sets out the purpose of Jesus' life as the writer understood it. He recognized that Jesus was sent for the marginalized, the underdog, the downtrodden and downhearted. At first the people praised his words but as their meaning sank in they became uncomfortable and began to undermine Jesus. They remembered that he was, after all, only the carpenter's son. When had he got all high and mighty? Who did he think he was, preaching to them?

Jesus went further by pointing out that God's servants are not always sent to those we might expect. A Gentile widow and an enemy soldier are examples of the sort of people to whom God offers grace. This was too much for the worshippers who did not want to be reminded of the scope of God's love, but rather wanted to hear about their own special place in God's heart. Time and again in the gospels we hear of Jesus' authority being challenged. At Nazareth the situation became very dangerous and Jesus narrowly escaped being hurled from a cliff. Luke offers a glimpse in this story of the life that Jesus is to lead. His willingness to follow the prompting of the Holy Spirit in obedience to God leads to derision, danger and death. Yet we know that the activity of the Spirit goes beyond death to new life, breaks the bonds of oppression and offers good news to the poor. Those of us who share in the life of the Spirit are called to proclaim the year of God's favour, to comfort the afflicted and to challenge the comfortable.

God who calls us

Prayer of approach

God who calls us together for worship:
Send your Spirit upon us.

God who calls us to bring good news to the poor:
Send your Spirit upon us.

God who calls us to proclaim release to captives:
Send your Spirit upon us.

God who calls us to bring new vision to all people:
Send your Spirit upon us.

God who calls us to work for the liberation of oppressed people:
Send your Spirit upon us.

Grant us the courage to proclaim that this is the year of Jubilee:
Send your Spirit upon us and anoint us in our service to you.
Amen.

Jubilee intercession

We offer God our prayers for the world and all people,
remembering especially those who live in poverty:

> parents who fear that they cannot feed their children,
> people living in refugee camps, temporary housing and those sleeping rough,
> people dying of curable and avoidable diseases,
> children unable to go to school.

Remind us that we have been anointed to bring good news to the poor:
Hear our prayers and inspire our actions.

We remember today those who live as captives:

> prisoners held because of their ideals or faith,
> kidnap victims and their families,
> those in the prisons of cruel regimes, facing torture and the death penalty,
> those imprisoned without charge or fair trials.

Remind us that we have been anointed to bring good news to the poor:
Hear our prayers and inspire our actions.

We remember today those who cannot see:

> people born without sight and those who become blind, facing the restrictions and
>   prejudice of society,
> people whose view of the world is limited through prejudice,
> people who are blinded by wealth, addiction and dangerous lifestyles,
> those who cannot see that they are loved and worthy to be loved.

Remind us that we have been anointed to bring good news to the poor:
Hear our prayers and inspire our actions.

We remember today those who are oppressed:

> people living in fear of violence and abuse at home,
> those oppressed because of their gender, sexuality or disability,
> people facing prejudice because of the colour of their skin,
> those who are not free to follow the faith of their choice.

Remind us that we have been anointed to bring good news to the poor:
Hear our prayers and inspire our actions,
that we shall proclaim the year of God's jubilee.
Amen.

Where all seems lost

Affirmation

In the wilderness, where all seems lost:
The Spirit of God is upon me.

On the journey, when I cannot find my way:
The Spirit of God is upon me.

In the market-place, where wealth defeats love:
The Spirit of God is upon me.

In the Temple, where tables are turned:
The Spirit of God is upon me.

In the Garden, when prayer is all that is left:
The Spirit of God is upon me.

In the flogging and the trials of despair:
The Spirit of God is upon me.

In the weeping, denying and fleeing of friends:
The Spirit of God is upon me.

On the cross, when tears are not enough:
The Spirit of God is upon me.

In the tomb, where death dances in delight:
The Spirit of God is upon me.

In the Garden, where hope's light is reborn:
The Spirit of God is upon me.

In the ascending, departing and peace-giving:
The Spirit of God is upon me.

On the Church I will pour out my Spirit:
The Spirit of God is upon me.
Amen.

May God's Spirit bless you

May our Creator bless you,
may our Creator bind you,
may our Creator bear you.
may Jesus bless you,
may Jesus bind you,
may Jesus bear you.
may God's Spirit bless you,
may God's Spirit bind you,
may God's Spirit bear you.

Amen.

Worship setting ideas

Place a table in a prominent position at the front of the worship area (it may be your Communion table), covered with a plush red cloth. On it place a large scroll. It needs to look important. At the point in the service where the reader/narrator describes Jesus being handed the scroll in the synagogue, hand the scroll to 'Jesus', who then reads it out (Luke 4.18–19).

A children's activity might include having sections of Luke 4.18–19 hidden on small scrolls around the worship area. Send them on a 'treasure hunt' to find the scrolls, and then get everyone to join in putting them into the right order.

Action ideas

Organize a hunger lunch to follow your worship. People pay what they might for a meal in a restaurant but are given a simple meal of soup and bread. Give the money raised to a charity that is working against poverty, such as Christian Aid or Save the Children (see page 143 and 144).

Consider having an audit of how accessible your church premises are for people with disabilities. Do you have large-print orders of service, hymn books and Bibles? Have you a hearing loop system, clear signs and good access for those with limited mobility?

Set up an Amnesty International group (see page 143) to write letters to campaign for the release of prisoners of conscience all over the world. This is a practical way to 'let the oppressed go free'. Continue to hold the people you campaign for in your prayers.

A prophet, not welcome

Hot, dry,
every day a battle
against despair.
I leave the now
strangely familiar,
oddly safe space
of arid sterility,
taking a risk
towards more fertile,
yielding ground.

Within me
burns
yearns
turns
an inspiration to change
myself,
the world,
those listening
to my God-inspired
no longer tired words.

Popularity
is not
an aim
worth consideration
but it oils
ministry's grinding,
squeaking axle.

I find myself
on old ground,
familiar faces,

older.
Wiser?
Take a chance,
be bold,
tell it like it is.

Can they take it?
Can I make it
matter,
important,
meaningful?

What's this?
Barriers,
I sense them
built high with derision,
suspicion for
one they
watched play
with scuffed knees,
climbed trees,
cried at splinters.

Anger,
stronger
than anticipated,
how quickly
hated.
Furious
self-
righteous
indignation
at a suggestion

that any
other
nation
might
fall within
the scope
of God's
love.

This is more
than
fear
of other,
this is fear of
the same.
That one
so well known
and locally grown
might know,
might grow.
Too familiar
to be heard,
cursed
and pushed
to the edge.
God
forgive them.

So that all might be blessed

An explanation of spiritual gifts

1 Corinthians 12.4–13

There are varieties of gifts, but the same Spirit.
There are varieties of service, but the same Lord Jesus.
There are varieties of activity, but it is the same Creator
who brings them to life in everyone.

Each person is given an experience of the Spirit,
so that all might be blessed.

To one the Spirit grants the gift to speak with wisdom.
To another the Spirit grants the gift to speak with knowledge.

To one the Spirit grants the gift of faith.
To another the Spirit grants the gift of healing.

To one the Spirit grants the gift of working miracles.
To another the Spirit grants the gift of prophecy.

To one the Spirit grants the gift of a discerning spirit.

To one the Spirit grants the gift of speaking in various kinds of tongues.
To another the Spirit grants the gift of being able to interpret tongues.

All these are brought to life by one and the same Spirit,
who grants gifts to each individually just as the Spirit chooses.

For just as the body is one and has many parts,
all the parts of the body, though many, are one body,
so it is with Christ.
For in the one Spirit we were all baptized into one body.
Jew or Greek, slave or free,
we are all invited to drink of the one Spirit.

We were all baptized into one body

Reflection

It is tempting to treat the passage from 1 Corinthians 12 about spiritual gifts and 'one body – many parts' as an easy commentary about Christian unity. We are familiar with the tone and the idea. We each have something special to offer to the life of the Church and we should be willing to offer what we have for the common good. But there is a stronger message here.

It seems that Paul is cross with the Christians at Corinth. They are allowing jealousy and prejudice to get in the way of their fellowship and witness. Some were boasting about the spiritual gifts they claimed to have received and using these to gain higher regard and status within the Christian community. As a group they were making distinctions between believers with a Jewish or Gentile background and between free people and the slaves that were part of the fellowship.

The writer makes it clear that this is unacceptable and demands a different standard from the people there. Any gift of merit will be recognized because it is for the 'common good'. If so it can be seen to be of God's Spirit. The Greek and Roman members of the group would have traditions of numerous gods and may have been claiming that their gifts were given by different 'spirits of God'. Paul makes it very clear that there is only one Spirit. Furthermore, that Spirit makes possible the baptism of all believers into one body. If all are part of the same body then they should be equally regarded and no prejudice of nationality or status should get in the way. The standard that God calls for in the Christian community is that of love.

We exist in a very different time from that of those early Christians at Corinth. Yet many of the things that Paul was concerned about have contemporary resonances. Jealousy and issues of status are still present within church communities. Expectations abound that the gifts of ministry are focused in the minister or priest, so that the gifts of others are not released or encouraged for the common good. The ethnicity of people attending churches can make a difference to the treatment they receive and the roles they are encouraged to play in the life of the church. The body is not one, but lies broken along lines of doctrine, tradition, prejudice and politics.

Can we rediscover the baptismal understanding of the Early Church? 'For in the one Spirit we were all baptized into one body – Jews or Greeks, slaves or free – and we were all made to drink of one Spirit.' This is as challenging a call to the Body of Christ today as it was to the Corinthians 2,000 years ago.

133

We come to worship

Prayer for gathering

Generous God,
we come to worship
each with our own gifts to offer to you and to one another.
Hear our songs and words of praise:
As we bless your name.

We come to worship,
each with our own concerns to offer to you and to share with one another.
Hear our silence and our intercessions:
As we bless your name.

We come to worship,
each with our own faith to offer to you and to strengthen one another.
Hear our passion and our prayerfulness:
As we bless your name.
Amen.

We gather in this sacred space

Hymn

We gather in this sacred space,
made holy by God's love;
and ask again the Spirit's grace
that faithful we shall prove.

We offer praise and humble thanks,
for all who've gone before;
for simple saints beside whose ranks
our voices now adore.

We seek to serve the present age,
to witness to God's Word,
to share the feast with child and sage
that love's true voice be heard.

As we receive these precious gifts,
signs of God's love and ours;
may grace again repair all rifts,
and break down hatred's towers.

Now may the blessings we receive,
be taken from this place,
that those we meet know we believe
in God's redeeming grace.

(Hymn in Common Metre, written for the 200th anniversary of Primitive Methodism)

Help us to remember the unity offered in Christ

Confession

We confess that we have failed to live as one body,
choosing to allow status, intolerance and misunderstanding
to create discord and disharmony within our fellowship.
Help us to remember the unity offered in Christ:
So that all might be blessed.

We confess that we have disregarded the call to love,
choosing to allow prejudice, jealousy and fear
to damage our relationships and limit our witness.
Help us to remember the unity offered in Christ:
So that all might be blessed.

We confess that we have been selfish with the gifts we have been granted,
choosing to use our time and resources
in ways that reduce life rather than enhance it.
Help us to remember the unity offered in Christ:
So that all might be blessed.

In silence we offer our personal confession.

Silence

Now you are the Body of Christ.
Know that your sins are forgiven.
Live in unity
so that all might be blessed.
Thanks be to God.
Amen.

One body intercession

Distribute paper 'body parts' to the congregation. Ask people to write on them their concerns and prayers for the world, the community, the church and in their own lives. They can then bring them forward, or stewards can collect them in. Stick the parts on a template of a whole body (a large church may need to double up parts!). Say the following prayer, or something of your own:

Loving God, you call us into unity.
We pray as your body for the world,
for our community, this church and for ourselves.
Help us to work together as one body in challenging injustice,
meeting the needs of others and building one another up in faith and love.
Accept these prayers in the name of Jesus Christ
and send your Spirit to inspire us to live as your people in the world.

Amen.

God who grants gifts

Affirmation

We believe in gifts
of wisdom, knowledge, and faith:
teachers, preachers, lecturers and learners,
students, pupils, graduates and reception class.

**We believe in God
who grants gifts
so that all might be blessed.**

We believe in gifts
of healing, miracles, prophecy:
doctors, nurses, midwives and health visitors,
prayerful people, activists and contemplatives.

**We believe in God
who grants gifts
so that all might be blessed.**

We believe in gifts
of discernment, speaking and interpreting:
careers advisers, youth workers and
    vocational guides,
speakers, comedians, linguists and interpreters.

**We believe in God
who grants gifts
so that all might be blessed.**

Bless each one of us

Generous God,
**bless each one of us.
Bless those we love.
Bless the homes we return to.
Inspire us with your Spirit,
that we might grow
    deeper in wisdom,
    more passionate in faith,
    more committed in our loving.
For the sake of Jesus Christ.
Amen.**

Worship setting ideas

Place attractively wrapped parcels on a display at the front of the church, representing gifts. Each box contains one of the gifts mentioned in 1 Corinthians 12. Invite people to open the parcels and show the congregation the 'gift' inside. Invite them also to consider what other gifts exist within your church.

Action ideas

Invite the Lay Witness Movement (see page 143) to lead a weekend at your church, helping you discover and develop the gifts within your church family.

Arrange a 'talents' auction, where the gifts that people have within your church can be offered to each other and the community. Lots might include a week's ironing, a night's babysitting, cooking a meal for four, etc. Donate the proceeds to a health-related charity, such as Cancer Research or British Heart Foundation (see page 143).

Offer the church premises to groups that hold fitness classes and encourage church members to attend!

I can, can, can't I?

To coin today's vernacular
I want to be spectacular.
Ordinary is not enough,
the everyday just seems too rough.

I want to walk across a lake,
see off a nasty slimy snake,
to raise the dead
up from their bed,
all this before the world's awake.

I long to do amazing things,
miraculously grow some wings,
cure cancer, heart disease, TB,
end infant death and poverty.

I need to use God's gifts for good,
bring peace into my neighbourhood.
Unite the nations,
resist temptations,
ensure religion's understood.

I know deep down I'm not cut out
for Nobel prizes and I doubt
that my deeds will save the earth.
Have my attempts so little worth?

Perhaps alone I'll not succeed
in getting every prisoner freed,
fairtrade winning,
conflict binning,
banning GM super seeds.

Are these your hopes, your fears,
    your dreams?
Work with me on these hopeless schemes.
One body, joined, we'll get things done.
Dance with the Father, Spirit, Son.

All things wrought in creation's birth
will move in rhythm with the earth.
There's only one thing left to tell:
that in God's love all shall be well.

(Fits loosely to the tune of the Cancan!)

141

Contacts

Details here were correct at the time of going to press.

Amnesty International
Working to protect human rights worldwide.
Human Rights Action Centre,
17–25 New Inn Yard, London EC2A 3EA
Tel: 020 7033 1500
www.amnesty.org

British Heart Foundation
Investing in pioneering research and support and care for heart patients.
14 Fitzhardinge Street, London W1H 6DH
Tel: 020 7935 0185
www.bhf.org.uk

Cancer Research
Leading funder of cancer research in the UK.
PO Box 123, Lincoln's Inn Fields, London WC2A 3PX
Tel: 020 7121 6699
www.cancerresearchuk.org

Christian Aid
Striving for a new world transformed by an end to poverty.
35 Lower Marsh, Waterloo, London SE1 7RL
Tel: 020 7620 4444
www.christian-aid.org.uk

Comic Relief UK
Vision – a just world, free from poverty.
5th Floor, 89 Albert Embankment, London SE1 7TP
Tel: 020 7820 5555
www.comicrelief.com

Contact – National Association of Child Contact Centres
Safe, friendly and neutral places where children of separated families can spend time with one or both parents.
Minerva House, Spaniel Row, Nottingham NG1 6EP
Tel: 0845 4500 280
www.naccc.org.uk

Eco-Congregation
Helping churches to make the link between environmental issues and Christian faith.
Arthur Rank Centre, Stoneleigh Park, Warwickshire CV8 2LZ
Tel: 024 7669 2491
www.ecocongregation.org

Hippo – the water saver
Every time a toilet is flushed the Hippo saves approximately three litres of water.
Hippo UK, PO Box 110, Ross-on-Wye, Herefordshire HR9 5YY
Tel: 01989 766667
www.hippo-the-watersaver.co.uk

Lay Witness Movement
Exists to strengthen churches in Great Britain, through spiritual stocktaking and encouraging growth.
Tel: 0115 8773827
www.laywitness.org.uk

Mothers' Union
Christian care for families worldwide.
Mary Sumner House, 24 Tufton Street, London SW1P 3RB
Tel: 020 7222 5533
www.themothersunion.org

MPH

Methodist Publishing House, 4 John Wesley Road, Werrington, Peterborough PE4 6ZP
Tel: 01733 325002
www.mph.org.uk

MRDF

The Methodist Relief and Development Fund makes small miracles possible for those living in the world's poorest communities through long-term development, emergency relief and campaigning against the causes of poverty.
MRDF, Methodist Church House,
25 Marylebone Road, London NW1 5JR
Tel: 020 7467 5132
www.mrdf.org.uk

NCH – the children's charity

Supporting some of the UK's most vulnerable and excluded children and young people.
NCH, 85 Highbury Park, London N5 1UD
Tel: 020 7704 7000
www.nch.org.uk

Peace Cranes

To promote peace, and in memory of Sadako, a young girl who contracted leukaemia because of the atomic bomb dropped on Hiroshima, people all over the world make peace cranes. Visit www.sadako.org to find out more and for instructions on how to make the cranes.

Save the Children

Fighting for children in the UK and around the world who suffer from poverty, disease, injustice and violence, and working with them to find answers to the problems they face.
1 St John's Lane, London EC1M 4AR
Tel: 020 7012 6400
www.savethechildren.org.uk

UNIFEM

The women's fund at the United Nations, supporting projects that promote women's economic security, human rights and status.
UNIFEM UK, PO Box 53247, London N3 3YW
Tel: 020 8392 3073
www.unifemuk.org

USPG

Anglicans in World Mission.
200 Great Dover Street, London SE1 4YB
Tel: 0845 273 1701
www.uspg.org.uk

WaterAid

An international charity dedicated to helping people escape the stranglehold of poverty and disease caused by living without safe water and sanitation.
2nd Floor, 47–49 Durham Street, London SE11 5JD
Tel: 0845 6000 433
www.wateraid.org.uk

Women's Aid

Domestic violence charity that helps over 320,000 women and children every year.
PO Box 391, Bristol BS99 7WS
Helpline: 0808 2000 247
Tel: 0117 944 4411
www.womensaid.org.uk

Women's Institute

Works to provide women with educational opportunities and the chance to build new skills, and to campaign on issues that matter to them and their communities.
National Federation of Women's Institutes, 104 New Kings Road, London SW6 4LY
Tel: 020 7371 9300
www.womens-institute.co.uk

Women's Network

The Women's Network of the Methodist Church aims to encourage, enable and equip women to participate fully in the life of the Church and in society.
Women's Network, Methodist Church House, 25 Marylebone Road, London NW1 5JR
Tel: 020 7467 5175
www.methodist.org.uk and follow the 'Open to You' link.

Index of titles and first lines

Index of biblical references